12 smart choices

choices

FOR FINDING

the right guy

georgia
shaffer

HARVEST HOUSE PUBLISHERS
EUGENE, OREGON

Cover by Dugan Design Group, Bloomington, Minnesota

Cover photo © Sashkin / Fotolia

Published in association with the Books & Such Management, 52 Mission Circle, Suite 122, PMB 170, Santa Rosa, CA 95409-5370, www.booksandsuch.com.

Based on *How Not to Date a Loser* with revised and updated material.

12 SMART CHOICES FOR FINDING THE RIGHT GUY
Copyright © 2008/2015 Georgia Shaffer
Published by Harvest House Publishers
Eugene, Oregon 97402
www.harvesthousepublishers.com

ISBN 978-0-7369-4940-8 (pbk.)
ISBN 978-0-7369-4941-5 (eBook)

Printed in the United States of America

14 15 16 17 18 19 20 21 22 23 / BP-JH / 10 9 8 7 6 5 4 3 2 1

To my mother,
Goldie Wise,
with love and appreciation
for all your support
over the years.

Acknowledgments

Writing this book was by no means a solo effort. I had the best team there is, and I want to say a special thank you to each one of you.

Janet Kobobel Grant—You are a true professional, and I'm grateful to have you as my literary agent.

Terry Glaspey—Thank you for your vision and enthusiasm for this project. You are a gifted editor!

Gayle Roper—I am blessed to call you my dear friend. Thanks for sharing your wisdom and writing experience and inviting me to attend your writer's critique group so many years ago.

Deb Strubel—Thanks for the millionth time. As I've told you so often, I'm not sure what I would have done without your editorial suggestions, support, and continuous encouragement.

Leslie Vernick—I thank God for your insightful comments, prayers, and for giving me the push I needed when I was stuck. I always looked forward to reading your suggestions.

The Lancaster Writer's Group—Month after month you patiently listened to each chapter, offering not only your honest opinions but your humor as well. Thank you for helping me to not take myself so seriously.

Linda Jewell—You are a real cheerleader! It's because of our conversation one winter's morning that I knew God wanted me to write this book. Thank you for sticking with me to the very end.

My Awesome Prayer Team—Your prayers made all the difference! My deepest gratitude goes to Penny Olivieri, Sue Smith, and the Living Word Community Church Women's Retreat prayer team. One day in heaven you will learn what I've already experienced—the power of your prayers.

Contents

Let's Journey Together

Maybe you read the title and thought, *Is there a right guy for me?* Perhaps you thought, *Will these twelve things guarantee I find my right guy?*

Or maybe you're wondering, *How do I know if I'm dating the wrong guy?*

I realize some of you may have reacted negatively to the idea of a "wrong" guy because in <u>God's eyes</u>, <u>everyone has value</u>, <u>worth</u>, and <u>purpose.</u> In that sense no one is or ever could be wrong. However, for many reasons, some people are not healthy individuals where they currently are. Maybe in ten years they will be, but not now. And the key word is "maybe." Here's a quick checklist to help you identify whether your current relationship is healthy.

Healthy or Not?

Place a check mark next to the following statements that are true. The person I'm dating generally...

☐ blames others (or me) rather than taking responsibility for bad choices and mistakes.

☐ prefers to stay the same rather than stretch, change, and grow.

☐ is stuck in self-pity and uses failure and loss as an excuse for lack of growth and maturity.

☐ tends to act out his feelings whether others are hurt or not.

☐ avoids pain at all costs.

☐ holds on to past hurts and resentments and has problems "letting them go."

☐ tends to hide the truth or is afraid to be open and honest about his feelings and weaknesses.

☐ focuses on self and ignores the feelings and wishes of others.

☐ feels threatened by any interests and/or activities you have that don't include him.

☐ perceives seeking the advice or help of others as a sign of weakness.

Scoring

1 to 3 check marks: You're probably dealing with the normal struggles of close relationships. We all have areas in which we can grow, and this book can help you do that.

4 to 5 check marks: You probably are involved in a moderately unhealthy relationship. This book will help you identity and overcome obstacles so you can move toward the joy of an intimate, loving connection.

6 or more check marks: You're probably involved in an unhealthy or even a destructive relationship or, put in another way, you are probably dating the wrong guy. Keep reading! This book may help you avoid years of untold pain.

In the context of dating, I describe the wrong guy as a "hurting person who hurts others because he lacks self-awareness and hasn't chosen to do the hard work needed to heal, change, and grow." A more practical description is found by contrasting unhealthy behavior with that of healthy people. What do I mean?

- Unhealthy people blame others. Healthy people take personal responsibility for their bad choices and admit their mistakes.

- Unhealthy people prefer to stay the same and don't see the need for change and growth. Healthy people want to learn and grow.

- Unhealthy people, like healthy people, have junk and sin in their lives, but unhealthy people make excuses for it. Healthy people work to overcome their problems and not be controlled by their pasts. They move beyond them.

- Unhealthy people stay stuck in self-pity. Healthy people bounce back from failure and loss, even when it's hard.

- Unhealthy people act out their feelings instead of talking or praying about them. Healthy people recognize and own their feelings.

- Unhealthy people avoid pain at all costs. Healthy people understand pain is part of living and growth.

In the first section of this book, we'll examine key areas that create obstacles in our relationships. We'll look at our dating histories, the fears that consume us, the blind spots we might have overlooked, the unhealthy patterns or lies we internalized from our past, and the losses that can keep us stuck. I'll share some of my own difficulties and those of other singles as you think about yours. By addressing these issues together, we can remove what hinders our healing and growth. When it comes to dating, what we don't know *can* hurt us.

In the second half of the book, we'll focus on the attributes and habits we can put in place in order to flourish in this single season of our lives and find the right guy. As you read about how other singles handled the challenges they experienced, please know many of the names and identifying details have been changed to protect identities. Occasionally I have compiled a single story from the accounts of individuals to highlight typical situations and positive solutions.

Each chapter ends with an opportunity to apply the information to your life and compile a "Smart Choice Relationship Profile." Many of these require thought, so give yourself the time you need for maximum benefit.

Once you complete your relationship profile, you'll have a record detailing your style of connecting to God, yourself, and others. Your profile will contain your list of deal makers, deal breakers, and intimacy blockers. Whenever you are in doubt about where you're going or how it's going, you can refer to your relationship profile and refresh your memory about who you are and how to make smart choices.

So grab paper and pen and let's get started on this adventure!

Part 1

How Did Dating Get So Difficult?

Reflect on Your Dating History

W hat was I thinking?" I said and laughed as I reminisced with my friend about a wrong guy I dated years ago. Long distance he looked even worse than he did then. I was married for 19 years, but in the ensuing years of singleness, I've experienced and made choices that now have me wondering, *What* was *I thinking?*

And in my counseling and life coaching practice, I've encountered some incredible stories that made me wonder, *What were they thinking?*

While most of us can laugh at some of our dating sagas years later, at the time it's painful when relationships don't turn out the way we hoped. And some dating experiences are so horrible it's difficult to ever find humor in them.

I can't tell you the number of hours my single friends and I spend discussing dating. Sometimes we express our pain. Sometimes we retell someone else's dating disaster. Sometimes we share the joy of dating. While each dating relationship is unique, it's amazing how many of our comments, especially about other people, end up being similar. You've probably heard them too:

He's so thoughtful.
He has a great sense of humor.
She believes everything he tells her.
Why doesn't she listen to our advice?
Why does she tolerate that abuse?

He'll never change.

The reality is that dating can be difficult, and there's no shortage of people to avoid out there in the world. We often meet them without even trying. One friend said, "If a wrong guy's out there, I'll find him."

As a licensed psychologist and a certified life coach, I've come to realize that it usually takes several failed relationships before we're willing to say, "I need help." Many of us allow our dating lives to just happen—to evolve on their own. We fail to consider that developing certain skills and insights may help us get better results or protect us from poor choices.

We're intentional about spending our money. We're intentional about doing well on our jobs. We're intentional about our health. But dating? I believe one of the main reasons we aren't purposeful here is that we don't plan on being single for a long period of time. We hope to quickly find that loving, long-term relationship, get married, and let our dating life fade into the distant past. Many of us don't want to be single, so why would we embrace what we don't want? And if we get good at being on our own, our season of singleness might last longer.

Another reason we may not want to spend time learning how to make smart dating choices is that it means we have to admit the truth. We're *still* single. We're one of *them*—you know, the ones married people say "have issues." But as my pastor admitted one Sunday from the pulpit, whether we're single or married, *we all have issues.* "And if you're wondering what yours are," he said, "get married and your spouse will be happy to enlighten you."

For years after my divorce I struggled with accepting my single status. The pain and turmoil caused by the separation and divorce resulted in some of the most difficult years of my life. I'll never forget my response the first time I was asked to speak at a singles conference. Although I spoke professionally on other topics, I said, "I don't speak to singles groups."

The meeting planner, who knew me fairly well, asked, "Well, would you at least be willing to consider it?"

I said yes, I'd think about it and quickly hung up the phone. Immediately I thought, *Well, Georgia, you* are *single. Why can't you speak to singles?* I suddenly realized I didn't want to speak to this audience because I would have to admit I was one of them.

I did change my mind, and that conference for singles became the first of many wonderful opportunities to reach out to men and women facing the challenges and choices of single life. Today I'm passionate about coaching people who want to address their real issues and establish healthy habits for love and life.

It doesn't matter whether you've just begun to date or your dating life is an ugly wreck, there's hope for you. You don't have to be an accident waiting to happen. By putting yourself in the driver's seat you can avoid crashing and burning. To maneuver safely through the hazards of dating, it's important to acquire the following qualities, much like a driver becomes adept at scanning the road and using peripheral vision to know what's nearby.

Be willing to learn. You don't need a college degree to be successful at meeting nice men, but you may need to learn new things and shed self-defeating behaviors. Choose to learn from your mistakes instead of repeating them. Work on gaining tools and strategies that will help you make real changes in your dating life.

The first step is to work on making yourself better. I know, I know. It sounds simplistic, but the truth is that the healthier you are, the less likely you will be to settle for anything less than the best. If you're reading this book, you've demonstrated you are willing to learn and grow. That's a great start.

Liz, whom I met recently while speaking at a conference, is a brilliant surgeon. But when it comes to choosing men who will respect her, she admits, "I'm pretty dumb." Many people discover that IQ and emotional intelligence (EI) are two different things. In dating,

EI is vital and, fortunately, can be learned. Daniel Goleman, in his landmark book *Emotional Intelligence,* states that EI is what enables us to be aware of our own emotions and gives us the ability to manage them. Emotional intelligence also enables us to recognize and handle the emotions of others. Improving your EI is one of many things you can do to improve your social life.

Be willing to stay connected. Caring, committed friendships, separate from any dating interests, are essential if we're going to make wise choices. Our relationships, beginning with our connection with God, provide the environment in which we can change and grow. Too often we ignore these close relationships to focus on that one special relationship—many times with disastrous results.

Back in my high school days there was a competitive spirit among some of my girlfriends as we vied for the attention of a few star athletes. What was lacking was a real sense of support for each other. As an adult I've experienced caring and cooperation, and I realize how vital this supportive mindset is to our ongoing growth and well-being.

"Authentic community," author and pastor Michael Cavanaugh said, "is people sharing their lives with each other. A sense of partnering with, a desire to be with, a personal interest in the well-being of the other person, a willingness to sacrifice for the good of the other person. It is what a healthy family would be like if family were available."[1]

Since family isn't available to singles—at least in the sense of husband, wife, and children—we need to create a network of people who are concerned about us and whom we can love and support. With our cell phones, iPads, and laptops, we're becoming more and more isolated and experiencing fewer face-to-face interactions that help us develop and maintain authentic community. We'll discuss this more later, but for now I encourage you to commit to cultivating a few close relationships. The best and most supportive relationship to cultivate first is with Jesus—who loves you and me unconditionally and faithfully.

Be willing to accept help. Sometimes the very thing we say will never happen to us does. When Sara started to date Tyler, she was aware of his history of jealousy and rage. "I can promise you—he'll never treat me that way," Sara said. As a capable, strong-willed woman, she had no problems stating what she wanted or needed.

As her relationship with Tyler developed, however, her self-confidence gradually diminished. When Tyler accused her of staring at or flirting with other men, she questioned her motives. She thought she'd only glanced at men, but perhaps she had really looked too long. Tyler undermined her relationships with her close female friends by finding fault with them. Over time she became isolated and Tyler became the center of her world. She loved him, and he controlled her.

"I constantly walked on eggshells, doing anything and everything I could to make him happy—to keep him from getting angry with me," Sara said. "But his jealous rages turned into threats, and then one day his threats became reality. I became a victim of physical abuse."

If you are involved with someone who is physically or emotionally abusive or who is addicted to sex, drugs, or alcohol, please seek professional help now. Abuse and addiction are vicious cycles you can't break alone. Ending a relationship with someone with these problems requires encouragement and support from people who care about you. We will discuss destructive relationships later, but for now let me clarify the differences between life coaching and professional counseling.

Life coaching, which is the purpose of this book, helps you gain the insights and skills needed to move forward and grow. Coaching often enables people to focus on and to reach their goals sooner because they have someone guiding them and pointing out what obstacles may be keeping them stuck. It also helps them become more cognizant and intentional about their own choices, actions, and feelings so that they are in a better position to find the right guy. In contrast, counseling focuses on healing from emotional pain and brokenness. Therapists might address issues from the past or a current crisis.

If you're involved in a destructive relationship or repeatedly trying to rescue and fix someone, be willing to reach out and get help. Sara did. She terminated her relationship with Tyler, and she's slowly regaining her self-confidence and rebuilding her life.

Be willing to be yourself. This book isn't about how to fix or save troubled guys. It's about you accepting yourself…and focusing on being the best you can be and making smart choices so you can avoid the pain and destructive behavior of unhealthy relationships. Too many of us pour vast amounts of time, energy, and money into trying to change or rehabilitate someone. Admittedly troubled people are usually those who have been deeply hurt or wounded and we want to help them, but, as the saying goes, "Hurting people hurt others."

To find someone who will help you be the best you can be as well as someone whom you encourage as he grows, you need to be real, to show your authentic self right from the start of your relationship. Recently on a flight home from Tennessee, a single man and I discussed the joys and challenges of dating. "The thing that drives me crazy," he said, "is women who are afraid to be themselves. They pretend to be someone they're not and invariably, after a couple of months, the truth comes out. Why can't they be honest right from the start?"

He's right that many of us try to please those in our lives and, as a result, we can morph into the person we think they want us to be. But as my seatmate said, sooner or later the truth of who we are is revealed. Pleasing people only produces problems, while being comfortable with who we are simplifies life. Plus it has the added benefit of making others comfortable when they're around us.

Be willing to commit to making one adjustment or change at a time. Many times when we commit to something new, we attempt to transform *everything* about ourselves overnight. Guaranteed failure! While everyone can use improvement in many areas, we need to be patient with the process. If we change too many things at once, we'll soon feel overwhelmed and hopeless and begin to believe the negative voice that tells us to give up because nothing will ever really change.

As you read the various suggestions and strategies throughout this book, focus on making one small adjustment at a time. Write the key concept down and put it somewhere you'll see often as a reminder until it becomes part of you. Once you experience success, make the next small adjustment. Slowly, over time, you'll see real change. I recommend keeping a journal or record of your progress. For me, it is often difficult to discern growth unless I can look back at what I wrote or thought months earlier.

Yes, you will make mistakes and experience setbacks, but as long as you are focused on making small changes, ultimately you will see a dramatic difference. Be patient! One day you'll look back with satisfaction at how far you've come.

Be willing to take a dating inventory. What is your dating history? Are you dating at all? If you have dated, think back on your past dating relationships. Go through your old journals, contact lists, address books, texts, or emails and list all the people you've gone out with more than three times. On your computer or on a piece of a lined paper draw four columns and label them with the following headers: name, attractive qualities, areas of concern noticed in the beginning (but discounted or ignored), and negative qualities that showed up over time.

Name	Attractive Qualities	Areas of Concern Noticed at Beginning	Negative Qualities Showed Over Time

Complete the chart by listing several people and traits. After you've completed your chart, highlight, circle, or underline descriptors listed more than once in each column. For example, are you attracted to someone with money or a prestigious position? Maybe you like business professionals who wear suits to work. Or people who are needy and want to be rescued.

Pay special attention to the list of negatives. You could get creative and use different colored highlighters to mark any repeated negative traits. While the positives show what you *think* you were looking for, the negatives speak louder. They say, "This is what I find. This is what I keep ending up with."

I've provided a few samples to give you an idea of how to be specific when completing your chart. (The names have been changed to protect the innocent…and the not-so-innocent.) The first one shows someone who was attracted to good-looking, kind, protective men, but she ended up with those who had anger issues.

Name	Attractive Qualities	Areas of Concern Noticed at Beginning	Negative Qualities Showed Over Time
Ryan	Kind and caring. Very protective of me.	Didn't even want me to go for a walk by myself in case someone hurt me.	Extreme jealousy. Possessive. Violent temper.
Jon	Well-mannered, beautiful eyes, exercised regularly.	Critical of waiters and those in service positions.	Critical and demeaning of me. Mood swings that included rage.
Garrett	Polite, great body, generous.	Demanding of those who worked under him.	Sarcastic. Wouldn't talk to me for a week if I made him angry.

Luke	Gorgeous. Loved sports.	Opinionated and inflexible.	Rageaholic. Rude and crude. Free time dictated by sporting events. Never showed affection.

In the next example, this woman was enticed by intelligence, competence, and great looks. However, she attracted controlling, driven men.

Name	Attractive Qualities	Areas of Concern Noticed at Beginning	Negative Qualities Showed Over Time
Cole	Brilliant, with several advanced degrees. Extremely competent at work. Knock out.	Obsessed with work and current projects.	Workaholic. Perfectionist. Detached emotionally. How people perceived him was of extreme importance.
Michael	Nationally recognized doctor. Stimulating conversations. Cute and wealthy.	Self-focused and manipulative.	Tense. Seldom relaxed or had fun. Critical and second-guessed everything I did. Focused on the image of being a successful doctor.
Aaron	Handsome, responsible, ambitious.	My feelings or opinions didn't count.	Control freak— his way or the highway.

By taking the time to consider your dating history, you may see for the first time the similarities in your previous relationships. Creating an awareness of the kind of people you're finding and dating is not to condemn yourself. Often after singles complete their charts, I hear, "How could I be so stupid?" or, "I'm so dumb." Instead of beating yourself up, affirm that you are doing what is needed to correct the problem.

Dr. Phil suggests that by doing a "relationship autopsy" and dissecting your relationship patterns, you'll get better at relationships, because you have the courage to be honest with yourself.[2]

Here's another exercise that may help you face the reality of the kind of guys you are attracting. It might even help you to laugh at the choices you have made. Barbara DeAngelis, author of *Are You the One for Me?* suggests taking the negative traits of those you've dated and writing an "emotional want ad."[3] Here are two ad samples.

> *Wanted:* Man who hasn't cut the apron strings with his mother. Especially looking for someone who hasn't grown up and thinks the whole world revolves around him. If you're the kind of person who thinks the rules don't apply to you, give me a call.

> *Wanted:* Handsome guy who needs someone to boss around. A lack of empathy is a real plus. If you love to use people and get irritated whenever things don't go your way, we need to meet.

One creative woman thought it would be great fun to have a small group of her close friends complete their charts and write their emotional want ads. She had a dinner party and asked each woman to bring a printed copy of her ad. She threw all the slips of paper into a basket and after dinner they read them. The goal was to see if anyone could identify the person who wrote the ad. They laughed and had a fun time. The game also confirmed to each woman as well as to her close friends the choices they'd made in the past and their willingness to now approach dating differently.

Each woman gave her friends permission to be truthful about men they saw her dating and point out if any of the men she spent time with "answered" the emotional want ad. Habits are hard to break, but having the acceptance and support of friends makes recognizing ingrained behaviors and changing them so much easier.

Not all singles have a dating history. Some have dated very little because they're waiting for that special person to suddenly see them, or they are shy, or they just haven't wanted to take the risk.

Makayla was infatuated with the top point scorer on her college's basketball team. She was bookish, slightly overweight, and shy around guys. Her friends were pretty sure she didn't have a chance with him, but that didn't stop her from spending hours fantasizing about what their relationship would be like when he finally asked her out. He graduated holding the arm of another classmate. Makayla realized she'd been so busy in her fantasy world that she'd overlooked the guys who had shown genuine interest in her.

Whether you're taking an honest assessment of your fantasy life or your dating life, the results may be painful. But awareness is the first step in uncovering valuable clues as to what's going wrong. These newly gained insights can protect you from poor choices in the future. Instead of mindlessly finding wrong guys, you now can be *intentional* about attracting healthy ones.

Coaching Tip

Using the top five most frequently listed negative traits of those you've dated, create a list of characteristics you will no longer tolerate in a dating relationship. Post these "Deal Breakers" on the refrigerator, on your treadmill, in a journal, on the bathroom mirror—anywhere you'll be sure to see them daily to be reminded of the type of person you've attracted and been attracted to in the past but for whom you won't settle in the future. Don't forget to also add this list to your Smart Choice Relationship Profile at the back of this book.

The Smart Choice Relationship Profile will enhance your awareness of who you are and how you relate with God and others. Gaining clarity about your personal style of connecting is crucial for building and strengthening healthy relationships. As one single said about the profile, "It's a fantastic tool! I really connected the dots for my own life and have reread it several times." Another person commenting on the profile said, "It was thought-provoking for me—especially the exercises on blind spots and intimacy blockers. They helped me understand how I relate to others."

Georgia's Deal Breakers

I will not continue to date someone who…

- is critical of me and demeaning of waiters, flight attendants, and anyone in a serving profession.
- is prone to extreme mood swings and rage.
- is controlling and manipulative.
- is self-absorbed, immature, and irresponsible.
- worships money, prestige, or anyone or anything other than God.

My Deal Breakers

I will not continue to date someone who…

- All from pg. 24

-

-

-

-

Smart Choice #2

Defeat the Fear Factor

*The wise man in the storm prays to God, not for safety
from danger, but for deliverance from fear. It is the storm
within that endangers him, not the storm without.*

RALPH WALDO EMERSON

One year at a singles conference I met a woman named Kathy who said, "I know Matthew doesn't treat me well, but at least there's a man in my life." After a long pause she added, "I'm afraid if I break it off with him I'll never find anyone else…and then I'll be all alone."

She went on to share that over the six years she'd been dating Matthew his verbal abuse had grown worse. He mocked her, her friends, and her faith. Although Kathy rarely drank socially in the past, she said, "Lately I seem to need a drink whenever I'm around Matthew." Driven by the desire to have a man in her life and the fear of loneliness, Kathy tolerates his poor treatment to her great detriment.

I would like to say my fears have never controlled my dating choices, but the truth is there have been times when I continued dating "Mr. Maybe I Can Make It Work" because I too was afraid I'd never find anyone better. I comforted myself with the thought that at least I had someone. Deep in my heart I knew this man wasn't the best choice for me.

Choosing not to deal with my fear made me more vulnerable to Mr. Wrong's positive overtures and more dependent on his companionship. Instead of addressing the fear that I'd never find anyone with the qualities I deemed important, I soothed my anxiety by continuing to date a questionable person. However, when I finally admitted this fear had a grip on me, turned to the Lord for help, and broke off the relationship, I strengthened my ties with God and was able to control my fear instead of letting it control me.

Psychologist and author John Townsend warns in a video series based on the book *Safe People,* "If all you have is a list of who to avoid but you don't address why you went after a relationship with them in the first place, you will continue to be attracted to them."

One of the reasons we're attracted to the wrong people is we're unaware that we're consumed by fear. This fear, in turn, often feeds feelings of desperation or an attitude of failure. But when we identify, expose, and deal with our relational fears about the future, we will be free of their crippling effects.

How do you know if your fears are influencing your relationship choices? Let's take a look at some of the ways fear adversely affects us.

Fear response #1: Changing who you are to be liked or loved by another person.

As one woman said, "I'm afraid I'll never find someone to love me, so I'm willing to be someone I'm not. I lower my moral standards and turn away from God's commandments." Her fears feed feelings of neediness and despair that will lead to problems and pain. Terrified that she'll never find someone to love her, she believes she needs to abandon her God-created self to find a mate.

Fear response #2: Tolerating abuse because it's better than being alone.

Danya and I first met at a singles conference where I spoke. We spent some time after breakfast on the second day discussing her current struggles with her boyfriend, her ongoing depression, and her declining health. My heart ached as I witnessed this beautiful, sweet woman agonize over whether or not to end an extremely toxic relationship. Several times she said, "I know I need to leave. I know he's not good for me. But he can be nice at times—really nice. I mean he's so smart." Then she looked at me and shrugged her shoulders. "I guess I'm just afraid of being alone."

Fear can prevent sound judgment. As Cheri Fuller says in *Trading Your Worry for Wonder*, "When we're preoccupied with fear and worry, thoughts become tangled. Worrying actually blocks logical thinking."[1] Most of us realize that losing a significant other who is damaging to our health and emotional well-being is a good thing. However, when we're consumed with fear, we don't think rationally.

Fear response #3: Not going out with someone because he might reject you.

Stephanie has been divorced for 13 years. She told me, "I'm so afraid of being hurt again that I say no every time someone asks me out. There's a gorgeous guy at work I'd like to go out with, but I'm terrified to say yes." Stephanie wants to meet someone special, but the thought of being rejected again has created anguish. She's right. Being ignored or rejected *is* horrible. If she takes the risk and he doesn't ask her out again, she will be disappointed or hurt. But being open and vulnerable to heartbreak is far better than allowing herself to be imprisoned by anxiety. Besides, there is always the possibility of things going well!

Fear response #4: Chasing away potential partners before they have a chance to hurt or reject you.

Because of being hurt by a few men in my life, beginning with my father, I feared being hurt again. When any man came into my life, I became extremely anxious—far beyond typical nervousness. Instead of handling my panicky feelings in a healthy way, I quickly tried to gain control of the situation so I would feel safe. Sometimes I said hurtful things or acted unkindly in an attempt to get the upper hand. My actions sent self-respecting guys running in the opposite direction. While these behaviors were nothing I intentionally set out to do, my anxieties controlled me. There were times when, instead of getting to know a person, I chose to protect myself by acting distant and aloof. However, my behavior eliminated the very thing I wanted—a close, intimate relationship with a godly man.

Fear response #5: Compromising your values to be with someone.

Emma's deepest longing was to be married to a godly man. As a Christian, she vowed in her twenties not to settle for any man who didn't share her devotion to Christ. But as the years passed and she watched her single friends get married, Emma began to worry. What if she never found a man with a strong relationship to Jesus?

During this time a cute guy named Jared asked her out. She realized on their first date that Jared was a marginal Christian who struggled with his beliefs about God. "But he had so many positive qualities that I decided I was being too picky," Emma said.

They dated for over a year, and about three months after their engagement, Emma realized she'd made a big mistake. Their spiritual incompatibility created all kinds of issues. Emma later said, "The pain of a broken engagement just about killed me. If only I would have stuck to my standards right from the start." With tears in her eyes she added, "Now I realize the painful price I had to pay for allowing my anxieties to dictate my choices."

Although Emma wisely chose not to get married, she is not alone in second-guessing her convictions. Many of us meet someone with potential and, pushed by our fears, we decide our previously set standards really aren't that important. We make compromises that in the short term look fine and totally acceptable. However, often months or years later either the real problems show up or we finally wise up.

While there are many more ways our anxieties can negatively affect our relationships, let's focus now on how we can minimize their destructive impact.

Minimize Damaging Fear

Our goal is not to eliminate all fear because not all anxious feelings are bad. It's in our best interest to fear reaching inside a hornet's nest. It's good that we're frightened to get into the car of someone we don't know or give our addresses to people we just met. These fears motivate us to do what is necessary to protect our health and lives.

The fears that send us into the arms of unhealthy people and keep us there and the ones that drive us away from what we want are those that we need to counter or eliminate.

We begin this process by identifying what may be fueling our behavior. I've found many times that just admitting to God what I'm most afraid of opens my mind to his wisdom and gives me a deeper understanding of what I can do to minimize the effects of fear.

Identify Your "What Ifs"

I hear "what ifs" from singles across the country. They often feel anxious about the future and ask, "What if the desire of my heart is *never* fulfilled? What if I *never* get married?"

Maybe you're like Hannah who, at 38, is starting to panic about her biological clock. She is haunted by these questions: "What if I never experience sexual intimacy? What if I never have children?"

Or maybe you identify more with Ashley. She poured all her resources into her career, but lately she's been struggling. She worries, "What if I can't pay my bills? What if I can't take care of myself?" When her close friend recently suffered a heart attack, Ashley became even more anxious. "What if that happens to me? What if I die alone?"

Our "what ifs" are as unique as we are.

What if I...

- can't make it on my own?
- die alone?

- get hurt again?
- lose my job?
- fail in another relationship?
- can't pay my bills?
- grow old alone?
- never have children?
- choose poorly again?
- tell him how I really feel?
- don't have money to retire?
- get sick and can't work?
- hurt someone again?
- never experience sexual intimacy?
- can't raise my children alone?

Consider what your top three "what ifs" might be. What causes you to feel threatened? What do you worry about? "What ifs" are fears of the future. Let's trust God for what's coming and be free in him.

Allow God and Others to Reveal Hidden Insecurities

Some fears are so entrenched we don't realize they are there. We've lived with them for so long they've become part of who we are. Usually during anxious or stressful times these insecurities come out in a negative way. Although such events are painful, we can learn important things about ourselves if we stop, acknowledge what happened, and choose to take action. Without analyzing and acting, our fears will continue to fuel our worst behaviors.

The singles group at my church was spending several days at a conference center along the Atlantic Ocean. There was one man, Brad, whom I especially enjoyed. One evening, as eight of us sat around the dinner table eating pizza, I turned to Brad and asked, "Are you going to help me write my book for singles?"

"Sure," he replied and smiled. "How can I help?"

"Well, I figure since I'm writing a book on how to avoid unhealthy relationships, you could give me some insights into the mind of a loser."

Yep, you read it right. After it came out of my mouth I couldn't believe I'd said it either.

Brad looked at me and shook his head. "Georgia, you're something." It wasn't a compliment.

Well, I couldn't sleep that night. Even though we'd all been giving each other a hard time in fun, I was shocked by my unkind words. I knew I needed to apologize as soon as possible. But the next morning at breakfast, Brad kept as much distance between us as possible (surprise, surprise). About an hour later, when no one else was around, we crossed paths in the hall.

"May I talk to you for a minute?" I ventured.

"What's up?" he asked coolly.

"I'm so sorry for the disrespectful comment I made last night. I could say I was teasing, but even then what I said was totally unacceptable. I hope at some point you will forgive me."

As I spoke, I could see the pain well up in his eyes.

"Georgia," he said in a calm, even tone, "just because you call me a chair doesn't make me a chair. Just because you call me a low-life doesn't make me a low-life. I don't know what men have deeply hurt you in the past, but you need to face your fears of being hurt again or you'll chase away every man who comes your way."

I stood there fighting back the tears. I knew he was right. The truth hurts at times. My disrespectful comment had been my feeble attempt to protect myself. Until that moment my fear of being hurt had controlled me in ways I hadn't seen or understood. But now it was exposed in all its ugliness. I'm glad to report Brad forgave me, and we are still good friends. I've thanked him many times for being willing to speak the truth to me in love.

How about you? Be honest. Do you say or do something negative when you're upset or anxious? Has more than one person made the same comment or observation about you, and if so, what was it? How did you respond in your meltdown moments? Consider what fears or insecurities your behavior could be trying to cover up.

Once we are aware of our deep longings and uncover those potentially destructive fears, we need to figure out how to handle them in a healthy way.

Develop Healthy Responses

Now that I'm aware of my tendency to act aloof or say hurtful things when I feel afraid or not in control, I consistently keep watch to replace my unhealthy behaviors with something more constructive. Here are some practical tools that help me...and will help you to develop healthy responses.

Focus on being proactive.
Focus on your options.
Focus on your blessings.
Focus on letting go. *of unhealthy behavior*
Focus on God's peace.

Focus on Being Proactive

Instead of dwelling on what could happen in the future, ask what you can do today that may head off your fears. For example, if you are tormented with the thought that you won't be able to support yourself financially, what measures can you take now to safeguard your financial future? Perhaps saving a larger percentage from each paycheck and investing it wisely may help you build a more solid financial foundation.

"Since I lost my job, I'm so worried I might not be able to support myself. It seems that's all I think about lately," my friend Alyssa shared.

"Well, what's one thing you can do now?" I asked.

"Besides working hard to find a job, which I've been doing, I can concentrate on cutting my expenses," she said.

As Alyssa searches for a new job, she can also seek help from a financial counselor. Once she finds another position, she could have a friend hold her accountable to save a certain amount each month. Alyssa is making the decision to be proactive instead of petrified.

But even if Alyssa does everything she can, there is no guarantee that her worst fears won't come true. None of us can control everything that happens. Therefore, it's also helpful to consider what we would do if what we dread becomes reality.

Focus on Your Options

Author and counselor Leslie Vernick says, "When my clients think through how they will manage or handle a devastating situation, they feel empowered. But if they fail to come up with viable solutions or options, they remain stuck."

Take time to reflect on questions such as, "What if I never get married or never get married again? What will my life look like? What are my choices? How can I live a meaningful life outside a marital relationship?"

Many times simply talking about fears with a counselor, friend, or coworker enables you to gain new insights and allows others to voice alternatives or different ways to approach the problem. As you begin to openly discuss your concerns with someone you trust, you'll discover options and solutions you may have never considered. For example, in the movie *Under the Tuscan Sun,* Frances struggles with the loss of her marriage and the realization that she has just bought a large home in Tuscany that needs lots of work. One of the fears she shares is, "What if I never have anyone to cook for?" What Frances quickly discovers is that she can make marvelous meals for the men she hires to work on her home. Cooking for them brings her great joy, and they soon become her new family.

Maybe your deepest concern is "What if I never have a family of my own? What if I never have a husband and children?" In chapter 9, we'll explore the importance of having close relationships and developing a supportive community, but, like Frances discovers, one solution is to create your own family with your friends, neighbors, and fellow church members.

Focus on Your Blessings

Often we obsess over the one thing God hasn't given us while minimizing or ignoring all his other blessings. Instead of focusing on your fears and "what ifs," remind yourself of all the things you appreciate about your current lifestyle. What are the positive things in your life? Make a list of what you most enjoy about being single. Place this list somewhere prominent to remind yourself often that your single life isn't a sorry life. Here are some ideas to get you started.

- You've grown closer to God. You are much more in tune with his "still small voice."

- You've become richer socially because of the time and energy you have to develop deeper friendships.

- You can relax and rest without upsetting someone's schedule. You can rest when you're tired.

- Without a spouse, you've learned skills you may never have thought you could do, such as lawn care or making home repairs.

- You can go on a mission trip without feeling guilty about using all your vacation time or the money it takes to go.

- You've learned God provides for you in difficult times. You've learned God will "instruct you and teach you the way to go."

Focus on Letting Go

A couple of years ago I asked friends and acquaintances for the names of people they thought were handling singleness well. I wasn't looking for people who felt "called" to the single life, but for those

who, for one reason or another, found themselv[
As I interviewed these people a few traits surfaced

First of all, there was a sense of peace about
they hadn't chosen to be single. They didn't feel l
current circumstances. They've learned to make the best of their situations. "There's a freedom in being single that you lose when you
marry," Lauren said. "You can do what you want when you want
without consulting a husband. I have come to enjoy that freedom."

Second, they openly talked about their struggles of letting go of
some of their deep desires and giving them to the Lord *before* coming to that peaceful place of acceptance. As one woman said, "I can
tell you exactly where I was on my college campus when I surren-
dered my desire to God and told him, 'If I never get married, it's
okay, because I'm going to trust you.'" This woman chose to believe
God loved her and knew what was best for her. She gave her dreams
to God. Even after her college graduation, when she found herself
struggling once again with the same issue, she continued to hold on
to the commitment she made that day.

I'm not suggesting you give up your hopes and dreams with an
attitude of resignation and decide, "Well, this is my lot so I might
as well get used to it." As Catherine Marshall wrote, "Resignation
lies down in the dust of a godless universe and steels itself for the
worst." Acceptance, on the other hand, "never slams the door on
hope." Acceptance says, "True, this is my situation at the moment.
I'll look unblinkingly at the reality of it. But I'll also open my hands
to accept willingly whatever a loving Father sends."[2]

Acceptance acknowledges that there is nothing wrong with the
desire to be in a loving relationship, get married, or have children.
But acceptance doesn't *demand* that these must happen to have a
fulfilling life. As singles we want to socialize, meet people, and live
our lives purposefully. We realize we can live with the pain of unfulfilled longings and dreams by focusing on what God has given us.

refuse to miss out on living and experiencing life. We let go of our wants and trust God.

Focus on God's Peace

Psychologist Daniel Gilbert, in his book *Stumbling on Happiness,* states that volumes of research have proven that though we're *sure* we know what will make us happy, the truth is we're often wrong. While we can imagine ourselves thrilled with a busy social calendar, a large bank account, a wonderful career, or having that special someone, the reality is we're making predictions based on how we *feel* right now. What we can't fathom with any accuracy is how we'll feel when we obtain those things. We may fantasize that winning the lottery would be a wonderful thing, but as some winners have discovered, it can end up being disastrous.

Dr. Gilbert writes about the reason for our erroneous thinking: "When we imagine future circumstances, we fill in details that won't really come to pass and leave out details that will. When we imagine future feelings, we find it impossible to ignore what we are feeling now and impossible to recognize how we will think about the things that happen later." [3]

While we may be convinced that if we're married and have children we will no longer feel lonely, depressed, or insecure, when it actually happens, we may discover that we are even lonelier or less secure. Maybe God's best, no matter what it looks like, is better than anything we envision for ourselves. As Paul reminds us, "Do not be anxious about anything, but in everything, by prayer and petition, with thanksgiving, present your requests to God. And the peace of God, which transcends all understanding, will guard your hearts and your minds in Christ Jesus" (Philippians 4:6-7).

Maybe you aren't experiencing God's peace because your fear is you've made so many mistakes God can't redeem your situation. If so, remember what the psalmist tells us, "O Lord, you are so good and kind, so ready to forgive, so full of mercy for all who ask your aid" (Psalm 86:5 TLB).

No matter what our fears may be, with God's peace and strength we can choose to deal with our anxieties rather than allowing them to control us. When we identify and expose our fears and prayerfully let them go, we discover we are no longer "needy singles" driven by anxiety and easily pulled into the traps of others. Instead we trust God as we look toward the future with anticipation and hope.

Coaching Tip

Since being accountable to those we respect helps us heal and grow, why not form a small group to help you process consuming fears? The group could use the following four questions that Rebecca Rice, therapist and leadership coach, uses with her clients. You can also use the questions on your own.

1. What is the main fear, concern, or problem?
2. What is the root cause? Where did it come from? What past event triggered this response?
3. How does my anxiety, fear, or concern connect with my current situation?
4. What is my plan to change my responses, including accountability?

Looking closely at your fears and anxieties, record your top three fears or "what ifs" in your Smart Choice Relationship Profile. You might want to refer back to pages 31–32 as you decide what thoughts and feelings create panic or feelings of uneasiness in you. Here is a sample and a list for you to complete.

Three Fears That Influence My Relationships

I'm afraid I'll be hurt again.
I'm afraid I'll fail in another relationship.
I'm afraid I won't have the money needed to retire.

Three Fears That Influence My Relationships

-
-
-

Smart Choice #3

Recognize Your Blind Spots

We do not see what it is that we do not see.[1]

DANIEL GOLEMAN

How did I miss that?" Katherine asked me. "Why didn't I see how controlling he was?" Then she added with a sigh of exasperation, "I feel like I have a big 'L' stuck on my forehead."

And she's not the only one who has felt like a loser. Many of us have wondered how we missed glaring traits in the people we've dated. Even if we did notice a red flag waving, often we discounted it as not being that important. Either way we usually ended up shaking our heads and saying, "How could I be so dense?"

When learning to drive, we are taught that there is a blind spot when we look in our side mirrors—an area where we can't see another car passing us. To ensure our safety, we learned it's critical that we turn our heads to look out the driver's side window and back.

Did you also know that we have a blind area in the center part of our eye when it's dark? Pilot, author, and vocational counselor Richard Nelson Bolles writes,

> When we were learning to spot airplanes in the dark, the Navy taught us that the center part of our eyes are blind at night. If you try to look directly at where the sound of the plane is coming from at night, you never will see the plane. If you look to the right or the left of where you hear the sound, you'll see the plane out of the part of your eye that isn't night-blind.[2]

You may have learned when driving or flying to be aware of your *visual* blind spots, but are you aware of any *mental or relational* blind spots? Psychologist Daniel Goleman, who tackles the topic of self-deception, writes that a blind spot is an appropriate metaphor "for our failure to see things as they are in actuality."[3] And it's those very things we don't see in ourselves and in others that can cause us to make unwise choices. While we can't steer clear of all dating disasters, we can keep them to a minimum by becoming aware of our blind spots.

Why We Fail to Notice the Obvious

The idea of mental, relational, and spiritual blind spots isn't new. The book of Matthew relates how Jesus called the Pharisees blind because they focused so much on their behaviors that they missed what was really in their hearts. Like the Pharisees, we can not only miss what's in our own hearts but also key character traits of those we know.

Dwight Bain, a therapist for 24 years, warns his single clients, "Before you get intimately involved in a relationship, you need to understand that one of the biggest problems is you will reach a certain point in the relationship where you will not be able to see what is there and you will *not* listen to the advice of others." He adds that premarital counseling can often be a waste of time because people are "unwilling to honestly see what's honestly there."[4]

It's crucial that we get to know someone to the best of our ability *before* we become emotionally intimate or consider marriage. (Yes, regardless of how much we know a person there are still surprises after marriage, but we should tackle any major issues beforehand.) We want to rid ourselves of wrong guys as early in the dating process as possible. Otherwise we're less apt to see or do anything about their troubling behaviors. So why do we fail to notice the obvious?

We're on an Emotional High

Attraction and chemistry are exciting. They energize us. We get swept away with emotions and fail to see things as they really are (note the phrase "love is blind"). One of the major ways judgment is short circuited is by becoming physically close too soon. Brain research indicates that having intimacy with another person causes changes in brain chemistry, particularly in women, that may cloud judgment and make it difficult to evaluate the situation clearly.[5] Dating someone once or twice and then being sexually intimate with them is a common occurrence these days, even among some Christians. *But having sex early in the relationship emotionally knits you together before you have the chance to know the real character of a person.* What recent studies are showing is that during sexual interaction a hormone—oxytocin—is released that promotes emotional attachment and feelings of trust. Our attachment to someone we barely know can put us on an unsafe roller coaster of emotional highs and lows. The highs have us believing this person is *the one;* the lows have us crashing to the depths of guilt, regret, and despair.

We might prefer to believe that the carefree sexual lifestyle portrayed on TV shows and movies such as *Grey's Anatomy* and *Scandal* is real, but the truth is we need to be aware that there *are* damaging consequences. Regardless of what the media portrays about having "friends with benefits," hooking up, or having casual sex, our emotional health as well as our decision-making ability is affected.

Unfortunately society appears to be blind to this truth as sexual encounters are becoming more prevalent, especially among college students. "Research is showing that between 40 and 80 percent of students have participated in a hook-up, defined as an unplanned sexual encounter between two people who have no plans to see each other again."[6] For Christian singles immersed in this culture, it's easy to be deceived. But as one married woman said, "Never, never, never have sex outside of marriage. I did this and tried to make it 'right' by marrying, only to discover I married the 'wrong' guy. I did this twice!"

We're the Exception to the Rule

We assume that the emotional experiences of others really don't apply to our lives. We think, *Hey, I'm different. The rules and research don't apply to me.* After all, we are unique, aren't we? God created us like no others. But as Paul reminds us in Romans 12:3, "Do not think of yourself more highly than you ought, but rather think of yourself with sober judgment."

"Science has given us a lot of facts about the average person," author Daniel Gilbert writes, "and one of the most reliable of these facts is that the average person doesn't see herself as average." He explains that many students consider themselves smarter than the average student, athletes see themselves as more talented than their peers, and drivers perceive themselves to be safer than the average driver. "We don't always see ourselves as superior, but we almost always see ourselves as unique."[7]

Self-deception is not the exception. And the mere fact that we perceive ourselves to be exceptional can lead us to conclude we'll be able to avoid the mistakes other singles make. Have you talked to sexually active singles about the risks of their behavior? While many Christian singles know they can't justify a sexually active lifestyle, they often minimize the risks because they perceive themselves to be unique. Sexual diseases, broken relationships, violent encounters always happen to someone else.

Don't assume *you are the exception* to this rule. You are like the average person in more ways than one.

We Believe We Can Change Them

We women are especially vulnerable to thinking we'll be able to change the people we're dating. We hold tightly to the belief that if we say this or do that, our guys will wake up, see the error of their ways, and change. What usually happens, however, is we end up disappointed and in a bind because of our illusion. As my friend Bonnie likes to point out, "There's one word for the married woman who is sure she can change her husband—divorcée."

As Elizabeth wrote in an email to me, "Before I got married there was a lot of tension and conflict between my soon-to-be husband and my family and friends, but I discounted it. I was trying so hard to change things and make the relationship work I missed all the signs telling me why it was not working." Today Elizabeth is divorced and realizes how costly it was to ignore that red flag.

We're Stuck on or Overreact to Past Experiences

Another reason we fail to notice the obvious is we don't realize we've fallen into the trap of overcompensating for or overreacting to bad past experiences. Whether we're still carrying around emotional baggage from an ex-spouse, a broken engagement, a death, or the family we grew up with, these unresolved issues impact our choices.

After her divorce Samantha questioned whether she was lovable. For years her ex told her, "You'll never find anyone else who will want to marry you." When Samantha began dating a man willing to make a commitment, she rushed to the altar. Later she realized her impulsive behavior was more about proving to her ex that she could find someone to love her than about getting to know someone and discovering what was God's best for each one of them.

Another way we overreact to experiences from the past is when a relationship goes wrong, we conclude we need to seek a totally different type of person. Instead of finding balance, we go to an extreme. I once dated someone who was laid back and unmotivated. When it didn't work out, I reacted by finding someone totally opposite instead of really analyzing why the former relationship fell apart. It didn't take me too long to realize that the focused and driven personality type has drawbacks too. Different is not necessarily better.

In the next chapter we'll explore how our childhoods affect the way we look at the world, but for now I want to mention that our experiences with our parents can be a key factor as to why we don't see things as they are.

We Prefer Fantasy

"When we got engaged, I knew in my heart something wasn't right," one single shared. "But the thought of ending our relationship was painful. I was bonded to the dreams of a new home and life. There was much to lose by ending the relationship, and the potential pain of the loss was sometimes overwhelming."

We often ignore an issue or pretend it isn't a problem because we want a certain future too much. Visions of white picket fences and happily ever after make us unwilling to go through the uncertainty and the heartache that come with a break-up. The reality of what we will lose can elicit tremendous fear and anxiety. While shattered dreams may be the price we have to pay to treat our current situation as it really is, giving in to our dreams and avoiding reality only create more pain for us in the future.

Before you assume you aren't holding on to any fantasies, ask, "Is there any truth I'm refusing to look at because of the pain and upheaval it may bring to my life?"

We Focus on a Few Traits

Focusing on the image or the package is what our culture teaches us. Is the one we're dating cool? Does this person have looks and personality? Will he turn the heads of our friends? Does he have the career, the car, the house, the prestige we want?

When we concentrate on only a few assets we especially like, we may fail to see him for who he really is. *The Bachelor* TV show is a perfect example of how glitz, glamor, and wealth can create excitement and infatuation that doesn't last. How many of those couples are still together today?

Even if we do see wonderful qualities in someone, we need to deliberately check for other traits or areas we may be overlooking or missing. For example, Carol's former son-in-law grew up in a dysfunctional family. He really fell in love with Carol's family, not Carol's daughter. After the divorce he admitted he'd married the daughter because her family was everything his was not—loving, successful, fun, and committed to Christ. He had found what he wanted in a family but ignored that he and his wife weren't compatible in many other areas.

We Forget "It's Not What They Say that Counts"

While we do want to listen to what people tell us, we also need to remember that actions speak the loudest. What do we observe in their daily interactions? How well does their behavior match up with what they are saying? They may say honesty is important, but do they fudge on their taxes or lie to their ex-spouse or friends? They may say they are caring and compassionate, but how do they treat people in service positions, such as waiters, housekeepers, and repair people?

For example, you might be having breakfast at a local diner that is short on staff. Two of the waitresses have the flu and the one left working is doing the best she can. Does the person you're with notice the waitress is having a hard time? Does your date have the capacity to feel someone else's pain? Or is it all about his own needs? We all show uncaring behaviors now and then, but watch for repeated patterns of disrespect.

While a car is a large object, we can miss it when it's in our blind spot and we're not paying attention. While "in love" feelings unleash some pretty powerful emotions, we must remain alert and ask ourselves and those we trust, "What issue or problem, if any, am I missing? What am I discounting because it's too painful to look at? What are my blind spots?" Then the question becomes, "Am I willing to make a change, even if it's a difficult one?"

Coaching Tip

To learn more about your relational blind spots and how to avoid their destructive impact, read my book on this topic, *Avoiding the 12 Relationship Mistakes Women Make*.

Look over the following responses shared by a group of singles and then create your own list of blind spots. What problems have you failed to see in the past? What have you ignored or discounted? (Don't forget to add your top three blind spots to your Smart Choice Relationship Profile.)

- Not looking at the true character of the person. Getting wrapped up in the surface things.

- Lack of mutual beliefs, lack of mutual interests, and lack of mutual goals.

- Controlling personality. Anger that is not truly justified, lack of self-control.

- He needed to be in a relationship. He has a history of leaving one woman and within a short amount of time he's right back in another relationship.

- One major thing I have not missed but ignored is the depth of the person's spiritual life. I tried to justify that it is okay just because the person is in church.

- Degrading me and treating me with disrespect in subtle ways.

Three Blind Spots I've Ignored or Discounted

1.

2.

3.

Minimize Dating Disasters

*Lord, may we have eyes to see, ears to hear, and a
heart to perceive what we may be missing.*

We love to have fun in the sun, but when we're in the water or surrounded by snow on a bright sunny day we can be blinded by the light. If we put on our polarized sunglasses, we can suddenly see things we couldn't see before. Polarized lenses minimize the glare caused by the light reflecting off the snow or water and protect our eyes from permanent damage.

When we're dating, we can be blinded by the bright possibilities of new relationships. It's so exciting, and the new person looks so good. If we fail to put on our "relational sunglasses," we may miss what's right in front of us and become vulnerable to the wrong guys. In order to compensate for what we might be missing we can pray, seek advice, pay attention to our instincts, and give ourselves time.

Pray! Pray! Pray!

Jesus warned his disciples about people who don't seek spiritual truths: "Though seeing, they do not see; though hearing, they do not hear or understand" (Matthew 13:13). In contrast, the disciples did search for the things of God, and Jesus said to them, "Blessed are your eyes because they see, and your ears because they hear" (verse 16).

Like the disciples, we too need to seek Christ and the truths of Scripture so that we have eyes that see clearly. We need to pray that the Holy Spirit—the Spirit of truth—will guide us and show us what we might be missing. God gives us this promise in Psalm 32:8:

"I will instruct you and teach you in the way you should go; I will counsel you and watch over you." Take time on a regular basis to stop, pray, read Scripture, and reflect on your life. Otherwise you're likely to miss something important.

What seems like many years ago, I was dating someone I really liked. It was going so well that my friends teased that I might want to subscribe to the latest bridal magazine. As the months passed, I knew I was becoming more and more attached. One day I wrote in my journal, *Lord, if this relationship is not of you, please show me.* Two days later this man called to say he really didn't see our relationship working out long term. He thought it best to end it now. I was shocked. And then I remembered my prayer. I admit I didn't expect God to give me such a quick and firm answer. Although I ached for weeks over the breakup, I knew God was protecting my heart and my future.

Seek Advice

God uses the people in our lives to bring to our attention things we may fail to note. We have an amazing ability to look for what we want to see, even twisting the truth if necessary. Wise counsel is a real blessing. The book of Proverbs tells us to "listen to advice and accept instruction, and in the end you will be wise" (19:20).

Emily dated a handsome lawyer and enjoyed every minute of their time together. It wasn't until they broke up and he started dating another person that Emily realized how she'd distorted reality. "I used to tell people he's such a good father and enjoys spending time with his sons. But what he usually did was take his kids to a sports bar and watch football with them." Rolling her eyes she added, "And I'd tell my coworkers he's a solid Christian when the truth was he only attended church with me."

While Emily was able to deceive herself, her friends had a much clearer picture about what he was really like. When one friend questioned her about whether he was really serious about his relationship with Jesus, Emily discounted her concern. When another friend commented on his integrity, Emily said, "I figured she was jealous because I was dating someone." It took almost a year and a serious incident for Emily to realize her friends were right about him all along.

Remember Elizabeth, who discounted all the tension between her soon-to-be husband and her family and friends? I asked her, "What would you want other singles to learn from your mistakes?"

"I think we need to be more open to feedback about the relationship from those closest to us who can see what it looks like from the outside," she said. "Asking for honest, constructive feedback can be hard to do and hard to listen to, but this could be a very important tool in stopping a bad relationship before it goes too far. Get comments from two or more people you trust. When all or a majority of your relationships deteriorate because of the person you're with, there is a problem. And this was a problem I didn't want to see." Then she added with a smile, "You can't just rely on your mom's opinion, although it may be accurate. It's important to get a broad base of feedback."

Friends, family, coworkers, pastors, and counselors often see the things we can't or have successfully ignored. Are you willing to open your life to a few safe people to obtain honest feedback? Gayle did. "I was happily dating Tom. One night my mother said, 'Gayle, I have to tell you I don't like Tom. Your father doesn't like Tom, and your brother doesn't like Tom. We have tried to like him, and while he's a nice enough man in his own way, we don't like him—especially for you.'"

At first Gayle was stunned by her mother's comment, but she also knew it hadn't been given hastily or in an angry or condemning way. She replied, "Ahh. I need to think about this." She considered what her mother said and today, 30 years later, Gayle is happily married to a different man.

Psychologist and author Madeleine Van Hecke says, "The most

direct path to discovering our blind spots is to intentionally bring perspectives other than our own to the table. This means that we absolutely need other people, people who are unlike ourselves, to help us see what we cannot see on our own."[1]

Pay Attention to Our Instincts

Even if we do get the approval of those closest to us, that doesn't mean we should discount our own intuition or sense about someone. "He said he was a committed Christian and didn't want to have sex before marriage," Natalie said. "He told me that more than one woman stopped dating him when she found out how he felt about sexual intimacy."

Natalie had met someone online and after chatting on the phone for a couple of weeks, they began dating. The problem was she and Anthony lived about 90 miles from each other, and the three-hour round trip limited the number of times they could get together. Since neither of them could afford the cost of staying in a hotel each weekend, after their second date he suggested she stay in his condo and sleep in his guest room for the upcoming Labor Day holiday. He even volunteered to sleep at his friend's house.

"I told him no," Natalie said emphatically. "I couldn't put myself in that position. It would be too tempting for either one of us." Although she had clearly stated her reasoning, she was confused by Anthony's negative reaction. "I don't understand why he got so upset. And why doesn't he get that I can't stay at his condo?" After pausing she asked, "Am I making too big a deal out of this whole thing? I'm really beginning to wonder if he just told me he wanted to abstain from sex until marriage to get me inside the door."

Natalie is right to be concerned and needs to be alert to the internal conflict she's feeling. There appears to be a discrepancy between what Anthony says and how he behaves. Did he give her a line to get her defenses down? Rather than make excuses for him or discount this incident, Natalie needs to listen to her gut and continue to carefully evaluate whether Anthony is "walking his talk."

Have you been around someone who "felt scary"? Beware! If your gut instinct says, "Run!" start sprinting as fast as you can. I had this experience once. One particular man kept talking to me. I suddenly felt distressed although everything seemed normal. Something about this guy was off, but I wasn't sure what. I felt the urge to run. Months later I discovered my instincts were right on. He had been convicted in a date rape incident. While we may believe it's unlikely that our social circle could include a murderer, rapist, or extortionist, it is possible. Criminals are often charming, socially skilled, and appear to be extremely successful.

Give Ourselves Time—At Least Four Seasons

When we're attracted to someone, it's so easy to get caught up in the excitement. As I told one friend who felt she was in love, "It's like getting hit with a tsunami. You need to pray you'll find a tree to hold on to so you don't get swept away by rushing emotions before the waters recede."

Although there are success stories of people who met, quickly fell in love, and have a great marriage, a far greater percentage of people usually say, "We rushed things. He wasn't who I thought he was. I had too little information before I made my decision to get married."

We need to give ourselves time to know each other *after* the emotional highs of a new relationship have disappeared. That's when the blinders start to come off and we begin to see each other's flaws, some of which could be major.

Time spent getting to know people in a variety of dating settings and situations is the only way we can learn someone's real character. People can hide who they are for a while, but given enough time and the right circumstances, the truth usually comes out. It's especially important to observe how he handles stressful situations, which won't happen if we only have lovely candlelight dinners.

How does your date react when you are lost on a back country road, the car breaks down, and he is hungry? Does he curse, yell, and throw things? Does he blame you for getting him into this mess? Does he take responsibility for his actions? Does he get silent and withdraw or does he laugh about the situation? Observing his behavior in stressful situations gives you another valuable clue to his true identity.

I've found doing remodeling projects together can be a real eye-opener. Once when painting a room with someone I was dating, I witnessed a frightening fit of irrational rage. While it only lasted for five minutes and wasn't directed at me, I was still shaking days later. It was the only time in two years that I saw that behavior, and it would have been so easy to make excuses for it—he was tired and hungry and having a bad day. (This was a one-time incident.) However, his family had jokingly talked about his temper, and I had noticed things like his unwillingness to forgive friends who had hurt him. Putting these clues together, I realized there was a lot of pent-up rage in this man. But I didn't witness his fury until the *second year* of our relationship.

Another suggestion I heard mentioned on *The Dr. Phil Show* about dating is that women can learn more about a man in an hour of play than in a year of conversation. And that "playing together"—engaging in a recreational activity such as rock climbing—helps to move the relationship along.

Relationship experts vary in how much time we need to witness deep character traits such as honesty, commitment, and integrity, but they suggest one to two years at the minimum. In the singles ministry at my church, we recommend at least going through all four seasons together. Vicki Scheib, a former director of a singles ministry, says, "In the eleven years I was in ministry, I've never had anyone regret dating through the seasons, but I have had too many people who regret not doing it."

Besides knowing character, it's important to gather information on preferences and habits. For example, how does he celebrate Thanksgiving and Christmas? Does he like to go on a vacation during the holidays or does he spend it with family or friends? If in a northern climate, how does he handle winter? Does he go into a deep depression or is he involved in winter activities such as skiing or snowboarding?

Even if we have to tie ourselves to a tree, we need to wait before making a major life commitment. Terri, who attends my singles group at church, said, "I tell my friends, 'Patience—patience—patience! Do not rush into a relationship. If it's worthwhile, it's worth waiting for.'"

Realize there will be things you won't notice right away in another person that could have a huge impact on your life. As one of my married friends likes to remind me, "Love is blind and you get stupid." He's right. Unless we put on our "relational sunglasses," we can miss what's right in front of us. We need to be willing to pray, seek the advice of others, trust our instincts, and give ourselves lots of time. Even if we can't see everything, we can rely on God: "Trust in the LORD with all your heart and lean not on your own understanding; in all your ways acknowledge him, and he will make your paths straight" (Proverbs 3:5-6).

Coaching Tip

How can we get better at looking beyond what we normally see? Let's look at some real-life examples of how we might miss the obvious. Can you identify with any of these stories? Remember, we want to be as wary as serpents and as harmless as doves (Matthew 10:16 TLB).

What was seen: "Sometimes he runs late, and I can wait for an hour or more before he arrives. We've walked into more than one movie after it started. I wish he would at least call me. I've asked him to do that several times."

What wasn't noticed: If you've asked him to call and he's ignored your request repeatedly, you have a pattern. Running late is one issue, but the fact he doesn't call to let you know he'll be late begs the question of how important your needs are to him.

What was seen: "I realize he's extremely jealous, but that's just because he doesn't want to lose me."

What wasn't noticed: Jealously is not love. Unreasonable jealousy and possessiveness can be indicators of a potentially violent or abusive relationship. Other signs include controlling behavior, isolating you from your friends and family, verbal abuse, and threats to you or those closest to you. Is this a person who doesn't want to lose you, or is this behavior signaling "Danger ahead!"?

What was seen: "I realize his anger isn't always justified and that he sometimes lacks self-control, but his parents were extremely abusive to him. Once he realizes how much I care for him, things will get better. I just need to love him more."

What wasn't noticed: Love and support are important; however, if he grew up in an abusive situation and hasn't dealt with those issues, the chances are quite high that you may be the one dealing with his pain. You are already seeing anger that is out of control. The *loving* thing for you to do is to walk away and refuse to tolerate this toxic behavior. Maybe it's not about whether you have the ability to love him more; maybe it's about his ability to receive it.

What was seen: "I know he occasionally looks at online porn—but that's just a guy thing. I mean, they all do it, don't they?"

What wasn't noticed: While some studies are showing 70 percent of men and 30 percent of women view pornography, that doesn't discount the fact that this behavior is destructive to healthy relationships. Pornography affects our ability to be emotionally intimate with those closest to us because we may prefer the fantasies instead of the challenges we face dealing with real people. Also pornography can promote unrealistic expectations, risky behavior, and even violence in some cases.

While most erroneously believe they can and will give up pornography when they get married or have kids, the truth is many discover they can't. Instead they are caught in a vicious cycle of addiction, compulsively seeking more and more vivid images to feed their craving.

What was seen: "I know he drinks a lot and can get carried away, but he's lots of fun. Everyone loves him. He said that once we get married and have children, he'll stop drinking."

What wasn't noticed: If he drinks too much, he may be an alcoholic, in which case you can't trust what he says—especially the part where he tells you he'll give it up once you're married. If you want your relationship to continue and be healthy, he needs to give it up now. If you don't see change very soon, and for longer than a few months, the chances of seeing real change later are slim. The fact that he's fun at a party will fade, but the pain of being married to an alcoholic will only grow.

What was seen: "He really enjoys buying motorcycles and things for his hobbies and seems to use up most of his disposable income that way."

What wasn't noticed: Maybe he shops to feel more powerful or secure and avoid problems. Maybe he ignores his responsibilities for play because he hasn't grown up. Or maybe his priorities aren't the same as yours. Are you certain it's only his disposable income he's using for his toys? If he is not fiscally responsible now, he won't be later. Do you want to be responsible for his credit card debt?

Overcome a Less-Than-Stellar Family

A child develops his sense of being as a worthwhile, capable,
important and unique individual from the attention
given him by his parents. He "sees" or feels himself reflected
in their love, approval, and attention to his needs.[1]

W. Hugh Missildine

We've discussed how healthy people attract healthy people. In order to avoid (rather than attract) wrong guys, it's important that we're not blind to any traits *in ourselves* that could put us in the questionable category when it comes to our ability to give and receive love.

We're all broken and damaged in some way because life on earth isn't perfect. But when we seek Christ's healing power and help from others, our lives are transformed. That still doesn't mean we're perfect. We'll always have areas in which we can grow. Even the healthiest among us have issues from our past that need to be identified and addressed so we can connect more intimately with others.

When we think about overcoming a less-than-stellar family background, we might assume this chapter is only for those who were emotionally, physically, or sexually abused. Not so! Even if we are from wonderful families, we have histories that left us ill-equipped in some ways. For instance, a friend of mine was confronted by her son:

> "I was abused as a child," Carter declared to his mother. At the age of 26, he was in his own apartment and successfully employed as a therapist.

"What do you mean abused?" His mother was shocked by Carter's outrageous statement. "We never mistreated you!"

"My home life was too easy," he said. "You and Dad gave me such a great childhood that I was buffered from any real problems. I never had to overcome anything so I would develop skills like resiliency—that's white collar abuse."

This may be an extreme example, but apparently most of us feel damaged in some way. One study of married couples in California found that 75 percent of the participants reported having had very difficult childhoods.[2] Although this survey focused on those who were married, most singles can probably identify with the feeling that our parents could have been more protective, less smothering, or more involved in our lives. The issue isn't whether we come from a perfect, loving, and supportive family as much as it is our *awareness* of the patterns and defining messages we learned in childhood that impact our relationships today.

We're not looking at our issues so we can feel like victims or blame and shame our families. Rather, our goal is to discover how our histories influence our thoughts, feelings, and the choices we make today. Instead of allowing our past to handicap us, we want to identify and work to minimize any patterns or intimacy blockers that hinder our ability to connect with others.

Intimacy blockers are behaviors, patterns, or habits that inhibit our ability to give or receive love. Asking three questions will enable you to uncover some of your intimacy blockers. To help you get started, I'll share my story using the questions.

What Was It Like Growing Up in My Family?

"Georgia!" my father yelled. "If you don't settle down, we're going to drop you off right there." He pointed to a large sterile-looking hospital-like building known locally as the children's home. "That's where they put children like you."

I had been picking on my little brother as we rode in the back-seat of the car.

Dropping me off at the children's home was a threat my father often repeated as I grew up. While he and my mother provided the basics—food, shelter, and clothing—I never felt loved or cherished as "daddy's little girl."

In our home, expressing honest feelings was not encouraged. When I declared at the age of five that I didn't want my parents to bring home my newborn brother, I was told, "You're a bad little girl."

At nine years old I sobbed when we moved away from town and I had to leave my friends behind. Rather than validating my loss, I heard, "You're only thinking of yourself. It's always been your father's dream to move to the country."

At my new school, I struggled to be part of the "in" group. Whenever I invited one of the girls in the popular clique to stay overnight at my house, they immediately declined. One of them informed me, "No one wants to stay at your house because it's so dirty and you live out in the sticks!" Then she added, "You have dead flies on sticky paper hanging from your kitchen ceiling."

I cringed. She was right. I hadn't realized that in the summertime not everyone hung specially treated strips of paper over their kitchen tables. Flies would get stuck to the paper and die. Our mud-tracked, cluttered home along a rural country road didn't even have indoor plumbing when we first bought it. It might have been my father's dream to live on a farm, but for me it was a nightmare.

The nightmare turned into a horror movie as my father experienced more and more pressure in his job as an electrical foreman in a large factory. On more than one night I stood paralyzed as I watched him repeatedly hit my mother.

I numbed the pain and all those feelings of rejection and insecurity by pouring myself into schoolwork. Although I brought home straight A's, my father always mocked my achievement with comments like, "Big deal. I work with engineers who got straight A's, but they don't know nothin'."

Our battles continued until I left for college. I called him "Mr. Know-it-all." He'd tell me, "You'll never amount to a hill of beans—and you can write that down in your little black mental notebook."

I didn't have to write it down because his words were seared into my soul. I determined that I was going to be someone, and that I was going to show him. I vowed no man would ever hurt me like my father hurt my mother. I continued, as do many of us, to keep that pain and shame hidden under achievements as I searched for approval. I was driven to succeed.

I now know, as an adult with a child of my own, the tremendous pressure my parents were under to make ends meet. I know how easy it is to say something in the heat of the moment that you later regret. I understand today that my father, who was either bipolar or extremely depressed, never got the professional help he needed. I realize too that he was a hardworking man who was exceptionally talented in his profession. But this knowledge doesn't excuse his abuse.

What Bad Habits, Beliefs, and Messages Have I Internalized?

The messages I picked up were, "I'm a bad little girl. I'm selfish and think of nobody but myself. I won't amount to a hill of beans." And those were just the spoken accusations. The unspoken messages were "men aren't safe" and "I'm not lovable, valued, or respected." I also feared, like my father constantly threatened, that if I made someone unhappy or mad, they would get rid of me.

It took me years and years to realize that no man, career, or stylish home was ever going to undo those messages I had internalized. Until I recognized the beliefs I had, examined them, and corrected them, I would continue to unconsciously live them out.

What Does Healthy Look Like for Me Today?

To overcome my less-than-stellar family, I had to acknowledge the pain I was carrying inside and the messages that were driving me. Then I had to ask the Lord to guide me toward healing and truth.

One of the first steps I took was to grieve the pain of not being loved and cherished by my father. Next, I had to forgive and let go of the bitterness and resentment I carried from childhood. (Processing grief and forgiving those who have hurt us will be discussed in detail in chapter 7.) Even after forgiving my father, in order to enjoy healthy relationships I needed to challenge the belief that I had little value or worth outside of what I could do for people. I had to discover and trust that genuine love and friendship aren't earned; they're given.

In the past I tended to date men who didn't treat me well. (One of my motives for writing this book is to help women like me.) Because men mistreating women was normal and acceptable in my family of origin, I felt comfortable with this type of behavior, even though I knew it was unhealthy. The idea that I'd be treated like a lady without earning it in some way was a foreign concept to me. To be healthy, I had to learn that by respecting myself, I was much more likely to be respected and treated well by the men in my life.

Recently I started to open the car door on the passenger side to let myself out, and the gentleman I was dating kindly said for the second time that night, "Georgia, let me get that for you."

I did, and as I was stepping out of the car I said, "As a single woman I'm in the habit of opening my own doors, but I really appreciate you doing this for me. Thank you so much."

"Georgia, I want to treat you like the lady you are."

At that moment I thought, *He's right. I* am *a lady, and it feels so good to be honored as one.*

Getting healthier and maturing in my relationships with men (I didn't have this issue with my girlfriends) meant that I needed to understand that there were some relationships (specifically the ones where the man treated me poorly like my father had) that I needed to either distance myself from or end.

I also learned that even the most healthy, loving relationship brings some hurt and pain, but it's a "good" kind of pain—like iron sharpening iron—something that causes positive change. If I don't get scared and run from that type of pain, I will grow. My childhood vow, "No man will ever hurt me," grew out of an exceptionally destructive relationship with one specific man. Not all men are unsafe.

If I'm not vigilant, it's still easy to slip back into the mindset that I need to be wary around men. Not long ago I shared with my girlfriend an email I received from a guy I was dating. After reading it she frowned. "I'm not sure I like his choice of words. I'm not suggesting you stop dating him, but I think you need to be aware that this *might be* an area of potential concern."

My knee-jerk reaction was fear. I thought, *I must end this relationship or I'll get hurt.* I was falling into my old, familiar pattern: Either I hurt you or you'll hurt me. I awoke early the next morning with a sick stomach. As I prayed and wrote in my journal, I realized I was overreacting. I was basing all my conclusions on a single email. I had slipped into the pattern of believing I couldn't relax around men, that I had to stay safe.

The good news is there is hope. Today I'm much quicker to recognize my fear and deal with any pain because I've learned that facing it makes me stronger. I have a much clearer picture of what healthy and unhealthy relationships look like. My friend and author Leslie Vernick says that all healthy relationships are characterized by some degree of mutual commitment and care, honesty, integrity, and respect. Unhealthy relationships, on the other hand, are when one or more of these ingredients are missing or not mutual. For example, if one person is dishonest, the relationship becomes unhealthy.

As far as that questionable email I received, I realized that only with time and prayer would I be able to tell this man's real character. Instead of struggling to control my relationship with him, which was my past pattern, I enjoyed our time together as I learned to know him better.

Keep in mind that we also have positive memories and patterns we've acquired. Ana, in my singles group at church, told me whenever her mother had a problem, she would immediately pray and seek wisdom from godly people. Ana internalized what her mother modeled and left that powerful legacy in the lives of her children. It's important to look for these positives in our families to keep things in perspective. For example, today I live in the country on a lot that was part of the farm my father bought years ago. I love it and am so thankful to live here now.

Our focus right now, though, is on what hinders our relationships. Let's go through the three questions once more using the experiences of other singles. This time think about not only what you learned or the habits you formed while growing up, but also those experiences that profoundly impacted you and continue to resonate in your heart today. We're all different and experience the world around us in unique ways.

My friend Betsy also had a parent who threatened to get rid of her. In her large Catholic family, her mother often threatened to put her in a convent if she didn't straighten out. But this never bothered Betsy. She said, "I never took that comment seriously. I'd tried to picture myself in a habit and thought, *That's never going to happen.*"

What Was Your Early Experience?

What did your parents, or whoever acted in a parental role, model about handling conflict? Did they avoid conflict entirely? Did they punish one another with the silent treatment? Did they shout at each other? When your parents had a disagreement, did they show respect for each other, listen intently, and work to solve the issue? Or did you see one of your parents blow up while the other shut up?

Matt said, "My parents ignored their problems, but later they would explode when some little thing triggered what was really bothering them."

Jenn not only heard her parents yell at each other, but sometimes their disagreements escalated to the point they physically hit each other. Katie, on the other hand, never overheard a disagreement between her parents because her mother didn't like it when people fought.

Perhaps your experience is more like Andrea's. She didn't have any clear memories of how her parents handled conflict. She knew her parents didn't yell or give each other the silent treatment. She knows they must have disagreed, but she has no idea how they dealt with it. White collar abuse?

How do you handle conflict? What creates obstacles in your closest relationships? What intimacy blockers inhibit your relationships? If any of the following traits affect your ability to connect with others (or them with you) in an open and honest way, write them down on your Smart Choice Relationship Profile.

Intimacy Blockers

- avoiding conflict at all costs
- failing to be yourself or not expressing true feelings for fear you'll be rejected or ridiculed
- physically acting out anger instead of using words and speaking with respect
- withdrawing
- giving the silent treatment to others
- placating or giving in to keep the peace
- having an affair to punish the other person
- blaming the other person for your anger

How did your parents handle bad times and loss? Did they acknowledge their difficulties and talk about their feelings of sadness and pain? Perhaps you saw one or both of them use food or alcohol for comfort. Maybe they shut down or became super busy. In some families, members learned that it's important to keep up the image that all is well even when life spins out of control. People are taught not to talk about "things like that."

Lily's parents always put a positive spin on everything. When her father had an affair, her mother said, "We must look on the bright side. Your dad has chosen to stay with us." Lily rarely saw her mother cry or communicate any feelings of betrayal.

When Gabby's father lost his job, he withdrew from family and friends. "My father as I knew him died. He just checked out." As adults both Gabby and Lily had to learn healthier ways of coping with loss so they wouldn't repeat their families' unhealthy patterns.

How do you handle loss and bad times? Do any of the following descriptors apply to you?

- numbing pain with food, alcohol, sex, drugs, work, busyness
- withdrawing from others
- pretending all is well
- refusing to discuss the obvious—"ignoring the elephant in the room"
- attempting to control everything

What did your parents model about rules and authority? Did your parents respect authority or did they criticize those in charge? Torry's father continually mocked Torry's basketball coach and teachers with comments like, "They have no clue what they're talking about."

Was your father a drill sergeant and your mother easygoing? Maybe your father was passive and your mother a perfectionist?

Jenn's father told her, "You will either respect me or you will fear me." Her mother warned, "You'd better not make me mad."

Do any of the following descriptors apply to you regarding the way you handle authority or rules?

- having an attitude of "It's my way or the highway"
- failing to set clear boundaries because it takes too much effort
- using threats and fear to control others
- disrespecting, criticizing, or demeaning authority figures
- going along with others without thinking for yourself

What did your parents communicate about love? Were they warm and open with their affirmations and hugs? Did your parents not verbalize their feelings, but you knew by their actions you were loved? Perhaps your parents reassured you with a comment such as "Of course we love you."

In Alexa's family there were no outward displays of affection, and she was never told she was loved. In fact, the message communicated was, "We wish you never had been born."

Liza was taught that love is a feeling that comes and goes. When she was eight, her parents divorced and told her, "We are no longer in love with each other." It was only as an adult struggling to hang on to her second marriage that she faced her trust issues. Liza came to understand that love is more of a decision and commitment than a feeling.

What do you believe about love? Would those closest to you say that you display any of the following characteristics?

- believing and acting as if love is a feeling that comes and goes
- believing and acting as if once love fades, it is over and nothing can be done

- believing and acting as if love is something you must earn

- believing and acting as if you're unlovable

- believing and acting as if people have little or no value: they're objects to be used

What Bad Habits, Beliefs, or Messages Have I Internalized?

Unknowingly Liza had learned that major life decisions, such as whether or not to stay married, are based primarily on feelings. When she no longer *felt* in love with her first husband, she incorrectly assumed the marriage was over.

Because Jenn's father spent most of his time outside of work with either Baseball for Boys, the Explorers, or the Booster Club, Jenn believed she wasn't valued because she wasn't a boy. Years later, when Jenn's husband physically abused her or spent all night at the bar, her parents ignored her complaints saying, "That's what people do when they've had a bad day. They get nasty. Let him go to the bar." To her, the unspoken message was she wasn't important enough to be protected.

For some of us it isn't what we learned as much as what we were *told* by those who mattered most to us. The list of messages that hurt and define us can be long, but here are a few you may identify with:

- Your brother/sister is smarter (prettier, stronger, nicer, more talented) than you are.

- Who cares about how you feel? You don't really matter.

- Be nice and go along. Keep the peace no matter what.

- Your opinion or feelings aren't as important or valuable as someone else's are.

- You'll never grow up.

- Good little girls don't do that.

- You shouldn't feel that way.
- You don't deserve anything good.
- Don't bother—you'll never get it right.
- It's all your fault.

What Does Healthy Look Like for You?

While we'll never reach perfection, healthy is being intentional about healing those past hurts and overcoming those lies so we can grow and lovingly connect in our current relationships. As children, our parents seemed so big and powerful. We didn't have the ability to recognize their flaws. We didn't understand that they, like everyone on earth, were damaged, broken, or disturbed in some way. Healthy is accepting their humanness.

In the article "Making the Most of Life, Even Without a Perfect Childhood," California psychologist Philip A. Cowan says that those who can forgive and put their less-than-perfect relationships in perspective by realizing that someone either didn't know any better or was doing the best he/she could do are the people who will "do better in their current relationships with partners and with children than people who are still angry."[3]

Healthy is realizing there are going to be times when our childhood patterns resurface, when we react to what someone says or does because of our pasts. We can often avoid that knee-jerk reaction or prevent further damage by getting still, praying, and waiting until we can talk things over with someone we trust.

In light of what you've learned about your family, what changes do you want to make? Jenn, whose parents screamed and hit each other, now says, "*Healthy* for me today is talking things out and not being afraid to express my opinions. It's also about praying and being part of a supportive community of people where we love and accept each other as the broken people we are. We are all in the process of growing."

Healthy for some singles is to take the first step toward expressing their honest feelings and setting clear boundaries. Isabella constantly tried to please others and had trouble saying no. Her boyfriend could pressure her into saying yes to something she either had no interest in doing or that was against her moral convictions. Healthy for Isabella was learning to set boundaries and say, "Please don't pressure me. I really don't want to do that." (If setting boundaries is also an issue for you, Henry Cloud and John Townsend have written an excellent resource on this topic—*Boundaries: When to Say Yes, When to Say No, to Take Control of Your Life.*)

Maybe healthy for you is seeking professional help to resolve a past trauma. A counselor can guide you as you deal with the hurts and help you break any destructive patterns. This will minimize the chances of recreating them in the future.

Yes, it can be hard work to overcome our less-than-stellar family backgrounds, but the benefits are worth the effort. I've found that when we heal from old wounds, our relationships become much richer and more intimate. And isn't that what we all want?

Coaching Tip

We discussed how our negative family experiences shaped us as children and continue to hinder our ability to lovingly connect with others. What are my parents like and which of their traits do I have? Ask your friends to help you see what patterns or habits may be creating obstacles in your relationships. Review the examples of intimacy blockers, look over the sample charts, and then complete your own. Don't forget to add your three most used intimacy blockers to your Smart Choice Relationship Profile.

Intimacy Blockers

- I don't communicate when something is amiss.
- I placate or give in to keep the peace.
- I believe love is something earned, not given freely.
- I'm unforgiving in current or past relationships.
- I'm unwilling to hear the truth even when spoken in love.
- I refuse to deal with issues that make me angry.
- I focus on "what's in it for me" rather than a spirit of give and take.
- I avoid conflict at all costs.
- I fail to be myself or don't express my true feelings for fear I'll be rejected or ridiculed.
- I physically act out anger instead of talking about feelings and speaking with respect.
- I withdraw.
- I give the silent treatment.
- I have an affair to "punish" the other person.
- I blame the other person for my anger.
- I numb pain with food, alcohol, sex, drugs, work, busyness.

- I pretend all is well.
- I refuse to discuss the obvious—"ignore the elephant in the room."
- I attempt to control everything.
- I have an attitude of "It's my way or the highway."
- I fail to set clear boundaries because it takes effort.
- I use threats and fear to control others.
- I disrespect, criticize, or demean others.
- I go along with others without thinking for myself.
- I believe love is a feeling that comes and goes.
- I believe once love fades it's over, and nothing can be done about it.
- I believe and act as if I'm unlovable.
- I communicate that people have little or no value; they're objects to be used.

My Intimacy Blockers

-
-
-
-
-
-

Smart Choice #6

Know and Live the Truth

Be a new and different person with a fresh
newness in all you do and think.

Romans 12:2 TLB

So you're writing a book on how not to date the wrong guy? Interesting. Well, I'd have to say that pretty much sums up my experience—wrong guys." Unfortunately, this woman's response, or something similar, is one I've heard more than once. The problem is she settles for less than God's best. She deserves better. However, what I think about her doesn't impact her life nearly as much as what she thinks about herself. What she feels is true affects not only the way she views herself but also the way she sees God and the world around her.

What we believe, think, and feel about ourselves influences how we behave. If you *think* you're a loser then you will *act* like one. And if you act like a loser, guess who you'll find? Hopefully you did *not* answer, "A vibrant, healthy relationship!"

On the other hand, if we think we're competent, lovable children of God created in his image, adjectives such as *inadequate, ineffective*, and *inferior* won't fit who we know we are.

Far too many of us singles hold tightly to erroneous beliefs ("I'm a failure," "I'm unwanted," "I'm defective") that we picked up somewhere along the way. These negative perceptions weigh us down, yet we continue to carry them not only from one relationship to another, but also everywhere we go.

There is no doubt that the abuse of my father—telling me I was bad and watching him hit my mother—made it easy to believe I was worthless and unlovable. Until I let go of those beliefs (they certainly weren't getting me anywhere) and replaced them with the truth from my heavenly Father, it was going to be impossible to see myself differently. As long as I believed I wasn't good enough, that I was undesirable, weak, and powerless, I would feel hopeless, angry, and depressed. I had to recognize that how I viewed myself colored *every* aspect of my life—from the way I saw God to the way I presented myself to others. If I wanted a fresh new life, I needed to see myself with fresh new eyes—with God's eyes.

What are some of the more common thoughts and feelings we tend to believe? One example may be, "I'm single because there's something wrong with me." For each statement we look at, we'll explore several questions. Is there any part that is true? What part is a lie? Is there another way of looking at this thought or feeling? What is the truth? What does God's Word say?

An important clarification: Satan likes to trap us with half truths. There is *some truth* to many of the erroneous things we've come to believe. Our adversary, the devil, deceives us by taking the truth and twisting it or changing it ever so slightly. Unless we are firmly rooted in the truth of God, we'll believe his distortions and think, *Well, that sounds right. Isn't that what God said?*

Jesus tells us lies come from Satan. He's the accuser and loves to condemn us. Some of us are fluent in many languages (maybe we can speak English, Spanish, and French), but Satan only knows one language—the language of lies. "There is no truth in him. When he lies, it is consistent with his character; for he is a liar and the father of lies" (John 8:44 NLT).

Keeping that in mind, let's look at some of the thoughts and feelings singles often believe.

I'm single because there's something wrong with me.

The reality is there is something wrong with *all of us,* whether single or married. We all have problems, and we're all flawed. But in Christ we are made whole. In him, we are lovable! And it's in him that our true identity lies.

The paraphraser of the Message Bible, Eugene Peterson, writes, "Since we've compiled this long and sorry record as sinners…and proved that we are utterly incapable of living the glorious lives God wills for us, God did it for us. Out of sheer generosity he put us in right standing with himself. A pure gift. He got us out of the mess we're in and restored us to where he always wanted us to be. And he did it by means of Jesus Christ" (Romans 3:23-24).

When Steffi told me she was single because there was something wrong with her, I asked, "Have you considered that maybe you're single because there is *something right about you?* Maybe it's because you've been obedient to God, trusted in Jesus, and haven't settled for anything less than his best! Or maybe a partner isn't in God's timing for you yet."

I'm single because God's upset with me. He's repaying me for my past mistakes.

Yes, there are consequences to our choices, and God does discipline us like a loving parent does his or her child (that's the part that is true). But we only need to read the story of the Samaritan woman who met Jesus at the well to be reminded that he also accepts us as we are (John 4).

Jesus treated this woman with kindness and respect even though he knew she'd had five husbands and was currently with another man. In her culture two divorces were considered a lot, so it is probably safe to say the reputation of this single gal was far from sterling. Plus she was a Samaritan. In Jesus' time the Jews considered Samaritans unclean people and never associated with them. Yet in spite of her past failures and her pedigree, Jesus treated her with compassion and respect.

I'm sure it was a bit unnerving to this woman when Jesus first revealed that he knew her history. But after her initial shock, it was probably very freeing to realize he didn't condemn her. He wasn't offended. He didn't tell her it was time she got her act together. That's not to say, though, that Jesus didn't desire for her to change and grow. He did.

I came to understand the healing power of acceptance several years ago when I was speaking at a weeklong event with several other professional speakers. At one point I was asked to talk with a woman who was extremely upset. People told me, "She keeps saying her life is hopeless, that's she's made too many mistakes, and she might as well end it all." Then one of the women reporting this rolled her eyes and said sarcastically, "No wonder she's so depressed—she's had several affairs with married men."

My heart sank. While I didn't discount that the lifestyle of this distraught single woman was creating problems for her, I also knew their judgment of her wasn't helping. Feeling overwhelmed I prayed, "God, what am I going to do? Her problems are too big. They aren't going to be solved in a minute. What can I do for her?" As I slowly walked down the hall to the room where she sat, I felt the Lord saying, "Pray with her. That's all you need to do. Pray with her."

I walked into her room, spoke to her briefly, and started to pray. I was so focused on my "God assignment" that I never even asked her name. I stopped praying, opened my eyes, and said, "I'm sorry, but I just realized I don't know your name." We both laughed. I continued to pray, and then we spoke briefly together before someone else walked into the room.

The transformation in her countenance was immediate and dramatic. I'd never experienced anything like it, and I clearly knew I had very little to do with it. She looked so visibly different that later several people said, "I can't believe it's the same woman."

God used me to communicate his love and acceptance to her in that moment. Nothing in me judged her for her adulterous affairs, and I believe she knew that. Now I'm not saying I'm perfect and there haven't been other times when I've been judgmental of others. This just wasn't one of them.

Like this woman and the woman at the well, Jesus loves and accepts each one of us, regardless of what we've done. To him we have value just as we are. When this truth permeates our hearts, we begin to see ourselves as he sees us—as persons of dignity and worth.

I'm single because my feelings don't matter to God. The desires of my heart aren't important to him.

Jesus knows the desires of our hearts. He does care, and he does want to give us what we want, but like a loving parent, he sometimes chooses not to. Sometimes we have to live with our unfulfilled longings as we grow or God works. That doesn't mean we don't matter or that God wants us to be miserable.

The woman at the well probably yearned for a man to treasure her and to provide a safe, loving home. Jesus knew these things would not fully satisfy her. He knew they would leave her wanting more—that fulfillment was in accepting him. And he wanted her to have more, far more—that's how much she mattered to him.

Jesus didn't give her temporary relief (a home and a husband). He offered her eternal satisfaction. He told her, "'If you only knew what a wonderful gift God has for you, and who I am, you would ask me for some living water!'...Jesus replied that people soon became thirsty again after drinking the well water. 'But the water I give them...becomes a perpetual spring within them, watering them forever with eternal life'" (John 4:10,13-14 TLB).

I'm a gardener. I live in the country and have a well. As any experienced gardener will tell you, there is a huge difference between the water from a well and the water that falls from heaven—rain. The latter nourishes my flowers like water from a hose never does.

This Samaritan woman also understood the difference between well water and the living water that fell from the heavens. As Jesus spoke, I believe she realized the gift he was offering her was far better than her own desires. He was offering her something that would quench the thirst in her parched heart and soul.

Jesus offers the same thing to you and me—eternal life and a personal relationship with him. He wants to give us something that will last forever. While we may not think this is better, and sometimes we may feel like he doesn't care about us, if we choose to believe what he tells us, we will discover new life in him.

I'm single because I'm so broken even God can't help or heal me.

All of us are messed up—that is the truth. Jesus meets us at our worst and transforms us into our best as he did with the woman at the well.

I imagine the Samaritan woman had plodded to the well in the intense heat of the day carrying all her pain and shame. But after her healing encounter with Jesus, Scripture tells us she *ran* back to her village, leaving her water jar behind (perhaps symbolic of all those burdens, beliefs, and lies she—and we—need to leave behind).

She not only forgot her pain, but also her concerns for the future and wondering how she could survive on her own. Jesus changed her, and now she was ready to change the lives of others. She had a purpose, and it was far bigger than her life.

I'm sure the countenance of the woman at the well, like the distraught woman I prayed for at the conference, was totally transformed. I'm convinced that she didn't even look like the same person when she went back to tell the people about Jesus. Her eyes sparkled. There was a radiance about her they'd never seen before. "Many of the Samaritans from that town believed in him because of the woman's testimony" (John 4:39).

With Christ nothing is impossible—and that includes healing

the damage in us, no matter how major or minor. He doesn't stop with healing us physically, emotionally, mentally, and spiritually. He transforms us so that we not only look different; we also think and act in new ways.

I'm single because I don't deserve to be loved.

Recently I watched the movie *Original Sin*. In this film Julia, with the help of Billy, marries a coffee plantation owner, Luis, for the sole purpose of stripping him of his wealth, which she did. What Julia didn't foresee, however, was that the kindness and gentleness of her husband would touch her so deeply she would fall in love with him.

Julia knew she didn't deserve this love—after all, she'd lied and deceived him. How could she trust that Luis's love was real after the way she treated him? As an orphan, the only sense of love Julia had experienced was from Billy, who grew up in the orphanage with her. However, Billy was extremely abusive and viewed her as an object to control.

When Julia told Billy that Luis absolutely loved her, Billy retorted, "No one loves you…no one could except me. Who do you think you are? You are a whore. You were born one and you'll die one. You have no future with him. Face the truth…let him go."

Julia didn't want to give up her dreams for a better life, but she was convinced Billy was right. She decided "she would never be worthy of [Luis]. She had to let him go."

After they drained Luis of all his wealth, Billy demands that Julia put rat poison in Luis's coffee. Julia protests but Billy tells her if she doesn't, he will. Luis overhears their plan, but pretends not to know. Minutes later when Julia puts the cup of poisoned coffee in front of Luis he tells her, "I've loved you, Julia. I love you because I know you…because I know you as you are…good and bad, better and worse. I've told you this already. You didn't believe me. Tonight you will know…" With that, he starts to drink the coffee.

At that pivotal moment, Julia understands that in spite of everything she had done to Luis, he loved her. Despite what Billy had told her, he loved her. Luis knew who she was, and yet he still loved her. Fortunately, Julia comes to her senses in time to save Luis's life.[1]

Many of us are like Julia. We realize we don't deserve anything better than the life we have. We're aware of all the mistakes and cruel things we've done. Like Billy, Satan continues to condemn us, telling us we can't or won't ever receive anything better. So we focus on and attract others who, like us, dwell on our negative traits rather than on believing what God has been trying to show us in countless ways—that he loves us in spite of who we are and how we act.

We don't have to do good things to earn God's love. In fact, we *can't* earn God's love! We only need to be open and receptive to his love, grace, and mercy. God is patiently waiting for us to believe and accept his love for us.

I'm single because God doesn't have my best interests at heart.

I hear this statement from many singles. One single gal in her thirties said, "I've been a Christian for years, and I've watched all my non-Christian friends find wonderful husbands and get married. What good is it that I believe in God? I don't feel like he has my interests in mind."

What about you? Do you believe you are single because it's God's best for you in this season of life? Or do you think God is withholding something good from you?

In her book *The Satisfied Heart*, Ruth Myers writes that as a young single woman, "I didn't believe [God] wanted what was best for me. I was afraid that if I gave Him the controls, He would make me do things I didn't want to do and I'd miss the best in life. In this time of rebellion I tried everything I dared, though sometimes the Holy Spirit blocked me. And I became more and more miserable."[2]

Slowly Ruth came to understand that God did have her best in mind. She said, "I discovered that the Lord could and did meet my deepest longing if I let Him be my first love."[3]

Just because we feel God doesn't want what's best for us doesn't mean this is true. Despite our feelings, we can choose to believe what he tells us. In *Having a Mary Heart in a Martha World,* Joanna Weaver wrote, "It was unbelief way back at the beginning of time that opened a doorway of darkness in a world designed for pure light…I believe Eve's eventual sin began with a tiny thought—a small, itching fear she was somehow missing something and that God didn't have her best interest at heart. What could be wrong with something so lovely, so desirable as the forbidden fruit?…Whatever the identity of the tiny irritation, it sent her looking for more. And Satan was ready and waiting, willing to give her more than she'd ever bargained for."[4]

If we don't think or feel like God loves us and knows what is best for us, we will recklessly seek "something more." We'll believe there has to be something better than our singleness. Like Eve, we'll take matters into our own hands, finding far more negative consequences than we ever bargained for. Instead of simply being single, we could end up being single and sorry.

Maybe we're single right now because God is protecting us from a troubling relationship. Or maybe he's in the process of bringing someone special into our lives—but it's going to take some time. Maybe his plans don't involve a special someone right now for us—or perhaps ever. Whatever our circumstances, we need to be honest with God and admit, like the father who begged Jesus to help his son, "I do believe [you want what's best for me]; help me overcome my unbelief!" (Mark 9:24). We can't allow the mystery or misery of our current circumstances to deter us from the certainty of who God is.

We've only touched on some of the thoughts and feelings that influence the way we see ourselves, God, and the world. It is my hope that you'll continue the process of identifying the lies and distortions you believe and do what's necessary to accept the truth that God loves you, watches over you, and has your best interest in mind.

The first step is to be aware of what you tell yourself or tell others about yourself. Just as we have to regularly scan our computer files and emails for deadly viruses, we need to be scanning and paying attention to what we've allowed on our mental and emotional computers. Ignoring a virus isn't going to take away its intent or ability to destroy our computers. Ignoring our thoughts, feelings, and beliefs isn't going to take away the impact they have to destroy or control our lives.

If we believe we're helpless and God doesn't love us, we'll act like we're helpless and unlovable. Anything that comes into our lives suggesting we can make a difference or that we're valued and wanted will be discounted or rejected because it doesn't fit who we believe ourselves to be.

On the other hand, if we see ourselves as loved and empowered by God, we will behave out of that mindset. We'll be open and receptive to God's love and to the overtures of friendship from good and godly people because, at the core of our beings, we believe God loves us and wants us to experience healthy relationships with others.

The truth of this recently hit me as I was shopping in an unfamiliar fabric store for ribbon. As I went up and down the different aisles, I crossed paths with the most cheerful little girl, about six years old, attempting to catch up with her sister and mother in the next aisle. She said to herself, "You have been such a good little girl. In fact you have been a good little girl for a whole year."

Initially, I didn't pay much attention to her words, but "You have been such a good little girl" kept echoing in my mind. Those words sounded so strange—so foreign. Just that morning I'd been berating myself for something I failed to do. With a scowl on my face I was telling myself, "You idiot. You put yourself in this pressure cooker situation. If only you would have…"

That happy little girl reminded me it was time to let go of my litany of self-condemning comments. Just because I was feeling like a failure didn't mean I was a failure. Yes, I had made a mistake, but next time I could—and would—do better.

Maybe you're having problems identifying what thoughts, feelings, and lies are causing you to see yourself and others in a negative light. If so, consider seeking the help of a godly friend, pastor, or counselor—someone who can help you see what is true and what is not. Be patient with yourself. Most of us struggle in this area at one time or another.

While my son, Kyle, was growing up, I often reminded him that we can't always rely on our thoughts and feelings to tell us what is true. For example, there would be times when he didn't think or feel like I loved him or that God loved him but—regardless of these thoughts and feelings—he could choose to believe that we did. Well, that tradition has continued into his adult years. When Kyle was in his late twenties he came home for dinner one night and as he was leaving, I said, as I have for years, "Kyle, God loves and I love you. You know that, don't you?"

"Sure, Mom," he nodded and smiled. "And I love you." Then for the first time he added, "Do *you* know that?"

I nodded my head "Yes" and fought back tears as he backed out of the driveway. After he'd gone, I broke down and cried because to this day I can still struggle with *believing* I'm loved and valued. But I *know* I am—by God and by Kyle.

Coaching Tip

Our experiences shape the way we view ourselves and the world. While it's easy to focus on the negatives that have happened to us, it's more important to examine what we continue to do to ourselves. It's time to uproot and remove erroneous beliefs. So remind yourself that *just because you feel something is true doesn't mean it is true.*

Despite what you may think or feel, you began the process of inner change when you chose to believe what God says. Ask those closest to you to help you identify the lies and the distortions (about self, God, and others) that you need to rewrite and replace. After you have identified them, write down the truths of Scripture that counter your incorrect beliefs.

When I was studying for my licensing exam in psychology, it was suggested that I study right before I fall asleep because that information would be repeated subconsciously throughout the night. Why not apply this same principle and read the scriptures you want to remember right before you fall asleep? In fact, you can tape a copy on your bathroom mirror to remind you of your affirming scriptures before bed.

Pick your top three lies from this chapter and transfer them to your Smart Choice Relationship Profile, because what you believe affects all your relationships. Here are a few examples.

I feel God doesn't want me to be happy, but here's what I choose to believe: "God is our Light and our Protector. He gives us grace and glory. No good thing will he withhold from those who walk along his paths" (Psalm 84:11 TLB).

I think God doesn't care about me or has rejected me, but here's what I choose to believe: "I have chosen you and have not rejected you. So do not fear, for I am with you; do not be dismayed, for I am your God. I will strengthen you and help you; I will uphold you with my righteous right hand" (Isaiah 41:9-10).

I feel I don't have enough faith to believe God will help me, but here's what I choose to believe: "Call upon Me in the day of trouble; I shall rescue you, and you will honor Me" (Psalm 50:15 NASB).

Here are a few more verses to get you started:

"The LORD your God is with you, he is mighty to save. He will take great delight in you, he will quiet you with his love, he will rejoice over you with singing" (Zephaniah 3:17).

"Give all your worries and cares to God, for he cares about you" (1 Peter 5:7 NLT).

"If any of you lacks wisdom, he should ask God, who gives generously to all without finding fault, and it will be given to him" (James 1:5).

Despite what I think and how I may feel, here's what God says is true.

Lie:

God's Truth:

Lie:

God's Truth:

Lie:

God's Truth:

Convert Pain to Positive Change

Will the pain destroy you or will it transform you?

A while back I ended a dating relationship with Mark. We had
gone out off and on for a few years, but we couldn't seem to
resolve some key issues. For me, no longer seeing him was a tremendous loss. I enjoyed Mark's company and hoped that somehow
God would miraculously change things in our lives so we could
make a relationship work. When I realized the truth—that nothing
was going to change between us, that it really was over—I became
depressed.

I had trouble falling asleep. If I did manage to sleep for a few
hours, I would wake up acutely aware of the ache inside. Here's what
I wrote during one of those lonely nights:

> It's a pain that feels like it will destroy me. It's a pain for
> which there isn't a painkiller. Everything within me screams
> for it to go away. I pray to Jesus for comfort—please, Lord,
> take this terrible ache away or help me live with it and
> focus on you.

The Lord answered my prayer. With the help of my friends and a
counselor, I was able to "go through," and most importantly "grow
through," the experience. I learned I had put too much stock in one
person. As I dealt with the pain and disappointment, I grew closer to
the Lord. However, the whole incident reminded me once again of
the reason why we avoid sadness and pain. It's a wretched place to be.

In the midst of this horrible pain we become especially vulnerable to the wrong person. We're tempted to search for anyone who

will ease or take our pain away. Someone who will hold us tightly and make us feel better—even if it's for a short while. Unfortunately, that kind of comfort is only momentary while the consequences are not. Until we take the time to heal emotionally, we will continue to search for someone to rescue us.

Whether the loss you experience is the result of a broken relationship or from missed opportunities, poor choices, or a difficult childhood, the fact is all losses need to be grieved. We can't make a fresh start in our lives, especially in our dating lives, until we first clear out the old. Grieving requires us to experience the heartache and all the feelings of anger, sadness, disappointment, and resentment. And how much fun is that? Right. So short term it's much easier to ignore the pain, stuff our negative feelings, and somehow numb them.

When my son was elementary-school age, he often complained about being disciplined for not following what he called "my stupid rules." Invariably, my response was "Kyle, I'm being short-term mean, but long-term nice." Choosing to grieve (and it is a choice) is similar. We have to say no to the desire to escape our pain in order to obtain the long-term gain of real healing and growth.

Kyle must have internalized that lesson because years later, while in college, he reminded me of the importance of pressing through the pain. His girlfriend had ended their relationship, and Kyle was heartbroken. As a typical mom I worried about him, calling him frequently, and taking him out to eat to make sure he was okay. I knew how sad he was. One evening as we chatted over dinner, I said, "Kyle, I know it's painful for you right now, but you have to press through the pain. If you don't grieve this loss, it will hurt your future relationships." (Why do mothers feel the need to mention things like this?)

Kyle, who was an All-American swimmer, rolled his eyes. "Mom, don't you think I know that? Every athlete knows you'll never improve if you don't press through the pain. It's the only way to get stronger and faster."

While strength and speed are not our goals in dating, the same principle applies. Pain and suffering can lead to maturity and strengthen our character, both of which lead to hope for the future (Romans 5:3-5). There will always be hurt and pain this side of heaven. Jesus warns us, "In this world you will have trouble" (John 16:33). To best position ourselves for healthy relationships, facing our feelings and grieving are a strength and a skill we need to acquire. Here are a few guidelines to what healthy grief looks like, along with some suggestions on how to gain from any pain you might encounter.

Grieving Isn't Only for Death

Sophia, who was 23 years old and heard me speak about growing through the changes we don't choose, told me, "I always thought grieving was only for the death of someone. I never realized that I would go through the process of grief with other losses as well." Many people erroneously think grieving is only for death, divorce, broken engagements, or significant tragedies. But any fizzled relationship, shattered dream, or disappointment is the loss of something that was important to us. With its death follows heartache and pain.

Even moving to another city is something we may grieve over. Although the move may be a desired one, it brings many losses. When Madison moved several states away she said, "I had no idea how devastating the experience would be. I've lost the ability to drop in and visit my parents. I've lost my church family and friends. I've lost my doctor, my dentist, and my hairstylist." Madison enjoyed her new job and slowly cultivated new friendships, but she also recognized and grieved over the changes and loss that came with her relocation.

Hitting the age of 30 or 40 and realizing we don't have children or the ideal family we wanted is something many singles grieve over. My friend, Abby, after her fiancé broke up with her, chose to purchase her dream home without having a significant person to share it with. "I grieved over the experience of buying a house by myself instead of buying it with my fiancé," she said. "We'd found a home we were going to buy together, and I'd dreamed about how I was going to decorate each room for the two of us. We were going to honeymoon in that house. It was a huge loss!"

Dating someone with "great potential" a few times can cause us to unpack our hope chest of unfulfilled dreams. As one friend said, "I've only gone out with him three times, but I'm already dreaming about a wedding on the beach." If on the fourth date my friend realizes this man isn't someone she wants to be with long term, she not only has to let go of the relationship but some of her dreams as well. Admittedly, four dates won't generate the kind of pain that four years of dating would, but it's still difficult.

We Shouldn't Compare Losses

Many of us play the comparison game. We compare what we experience to the suffering of someone else and think, *Well, it could be worse. My relationship ended after two months, but she's facing a broken engagement.* Or we think, *He's lost his job and home. I've only lost a promised promotion.* Because we can always find someone with a more tragic situation, we end up discounting or minimizing the void that exists in our lives.

But our pain is our pain—even if it's over something that's not as life-shattering as someone else's heartache. If we minimize it instead of face it, we're more apt to discount the need to grieve, telling ourselves that our loss isn't significant enough or our pain isn't great enough. And many times those closest to us question why we feel so sad. "After all," they tell us, "it could be worse." This doesn't help!

Meredith chose to end her relationship with Jacob because she realized after months of dating that he didn't share her values. She was on fire for the Lord while Jacob basically showed up at church on Sundays and went through the motions. Because they'd enjoyed many fun evenings together, she missed his friendship. Besides, he did have lots of wonderful qualities. One evening as she cried over the phone to a friend about the end of her relationship with Jacob, her friend said, "Meredith! You're the one who broke up with him. I don't understand why *you* are so upset."

Meredith's friend was comparing Meredith's pain of breaking up with someone by choice with the pain of being broken up with. While the pain of rejection is added to the pain of loss when it's not your choice, both situations are painful. Meredith was hurting, and comparing her loss to someone else's experience didn't validate how she felt.

In Ecclesiastes 3:4 we are reminded that there is "a time to weep and a time to laugh, a time to mourn and a time to dance." It doesn't matter what issue has left us heartbroken, whether it's a loss from a choice we made or a choice that was made for us. We need to recognize that for us the pain is real, and we must grieve so we can heal and move forward emotionally healthy.

Anger and Sadness Are Part of Grief

"I felt angry with everyone, especially God," Robyn said after her two-year marriage ended. "To me God felt like a mean monster that enjoyed seeing me suffer. It took me months to let go of my bitterness and resentment." Anger and rage are common reactions to loss. The problem isn't that we get angry as much as what we do with our anger. Paul reminds us, "In your anger do not sin" (Ephesians 4:6).

To avoid the damage and hurt anger can cause to us and others, we need to first be willing to acknowledge our anger and then do something constructive with it. Life coach and counselor Dwight Bain tells his clients they have two choices: "You can either cry out or act out."

"Crying out" means we turn to God and others as we face and pour out our deep hurts. We can ask God for his perspective on our situation: "Lord, how do you want me to respond to this?" or "How do you want me to see this?" We can write in a journal, unloading our deep hurts and frustrations. We may choose to talk to a counselor or a caring friend—someone who is a good listener and willing to help us or let us express our emotions.

"Acting out" is when we ignore or discount the problem, which allows it to be bottled up. Or we let the emotion control us. Then we thoughtlessly say or do something (either now or later) that is destructive to us and others.

In the healthy choice, once we're aware of the anger and bitterness and have "cried out," we need to *choose* to forgive and work toward letting go of lingering resentments. Holding on to them comes naturally; letting go takes real inner strength and help from God.

When we forgive, we're not saying what someone did to us was okay. For instance, it is not acceptable that an ex-boyfriend consistently cut you down with his vicious words. His critical comments were demeaning and cost you a great deal of heartache and pain. Forgiving means acknowledging what was done, who did it, and how we felt as a result of that experience. We then *ask God* to lead us toward healing and forgiveness so we can be free to move on.

Forgiveness usually isn't a "once and done" experience. Depending on what happened, it can be a long process. In fact, when you think you are at the point of finally letting go, something can happen to set off feelings of bitterness and rage all over again. Stay in the process because there is tremendous healing power in forgiveness!

Grieving Means Cooperating with the Pain

Loss depletes our mental, emotional, and physical resources. The most routine tasks become difficult. Decision making can be overwhelming. When Abby's engagement abruptly ended, the intense emotional pain she experienced interfered with everything in her life. She had problems focusing at work, she had little energy for friends on weekends, and she was constantly nagged with questions such as "What's wrong with me?" She spent many hours over the next few months crying, praying, and talking with a counselor and a few caring friends. She filled the pages in her journal with her thoughts and feelings. She wrote about what she believed the "pain" was telling her and teaching her. It was almost a year later when Abby was finally able to recover from her loss and move on.

What benefits did she gain by cooperating with the pain and carving out time to grieve? "I now know that much of the pain was inside—not outside—of me," Abby shared. "I kept looking for or hoping that someone would rescue me and take me out of my pain. When that didn't happen, I drew closer to God and discovered his comfort in the midst of it all. I allowed Jesus to fill the emptiness that was inside of me."

Abby realized how much she'd grown through the process when one of her closest friends became engaged. "Because I wasn't so empty myself," she said, "I could honestly be thrilled for Jillian and celebrate her upcoming wedding."

Like Abby did, we need to give ourselves permission to rest and renew our depleted resources after loss. Instead of pushing yourself when you feel washed out, ask, "What commitments or activities can I cut back on or eliminate for a while?" And find a way, such as journaling, to reflect on what has happened, sort through your emotions, and maybe even reprioritize your life.

No Painkillers Available

There are times when the aches in our souls are so deep and crippling that we wonder, *Why does this hurt so much?* Because we live in a culture that believes if there is a pain, there is a cure for it, we often have the mentality that there has to be something to lessen our discomfort or misery. In his book *Shattered Dreams*, Larry Crabb writes, "People who find some way to deaden their pain never discover their desire for God in all its fullness." He says that the kind of pain that is inconsolable will "carry us into the inner recesses of our being that wants God. If we deny how badly we hurt, we remain unaware of our desire for God."[1]

When the intense pain threatens to destroy us, we want to face it, be honest about it, and cry out to God. A couple more options that may help deal with the gnawing ache inside are writing about it, finding other activities to participate in, and incorporating more of God's Word in your life.

Write or Journal

Earlier I talked about my son Kyle's depression after a breakup in college. One of the ways he expressed his feelings was to write. He penned this poem:

> I remember the days long ago
> When things were beautiful like a sunset glow
> But now the days seem dark and bare
> And I walk alone with no one to share
> The light from my eyes is all but gone
> And I want to leave but I can't move on
> Just thinking about you makes me sad
> How someone so beautiful I once had
> It's not your fault you had to leave
> And I want you back but I won't plead
> You touched my heart in so many ways
> And the minutes that pass seem like days
> So I did the best thing that I could do
> I picked up a pen and wrote about you
> And all those memories we did share
> Like at States when you were there
> And when I did poorly at Nationals I could have cried
> But your voice kept me from falling apart inside
> All those times you were there for me
> And seeing your smile always set me free
> I'll never regret you being a part of my life
> And I know someday you will make a wonderful wife
> So in closing I have this to say
> May God bless you each and every day.[2]

Enjoy a Hobby or Sport

Gardening has been and continues to be a valuable outlet for me. As I pull out the weeds, I mentally remove whatever negative emotions are seething inside of me. As I trim the straggly growth on my rose arbor, I consider what needs to be trimmed in my life.

What helps you sort through and process your pain? Do you like to exercise, bike, bake, clean? Do you like to play the cello, mountain climb, or volunteer to help youngsters learn to read? What helps you manage your emotions rather than carry them inside?

Hold on to Scripture

During difficult times the Word of God encourages us and gives us hope. What scriptures have helped you in the past? I've written mine in a special journal, and I've also put them on index cards I keep on the table next to my bed. When I face a painful situation, I reach for those cards to give me comfort and help me focus on God rather than the problem. Scripture is a continual reminder that God is still in control.

Here are two that remind me of the value of crying out to God:

> Call upon me in the day of trouble; I will deliver you, and you will honor me (Psalm 50:15).

> O LORD my God, I called to you for help and you healed me (Psalm 30:2).

These two are helpful when I'm working too hard to change a difficult situation:

> Be still and know that I am God (Psalm 46:10).

> This is what the Sovereign LORD, the Holy One of Israel, says: "In repentance and rest is your salvation, in quietness and trust is your strength" (Isaiah 30:15).

This verse reminds me that in the midst of the gnawing pain I can still experience the comfort of God:

> Praise be to the God and Father of our Lord Jesus Christ, the Father of compassion and the God of all comfort, who comforts us in all our troubles (2 Corinthians 1:3-4).

A single friend said,

> I wrote down every [scripture] "promise" I could find on index cards and plastered them all over the door in my kitchen. Then, when I moved, I created a collage of sorts as I posted them above my bed so it looks like a funky headboard. Since I generally sleep when I'm feeling down, it's the first thing I see as I head toward the bed, so I can sit and read over those verses before going to sleep. I've found it helpful to remind myself that God is in control, especially when my world seems like it's falling apart.

Grief Lasts Longer Than We Expect

Although Nicole's engagement had ended six months earlier, she was confused as to why she still wasn't her old self. "Why am I still dragging myself to work? Why isn't it easier by now?"

There are at least three reasons why grieving takes longer than we expect or have the patience for. First, there is the initial shock, numbness, and disbelief that often come when we first encounter an unexpected event. Depending on what happened, it can take 6 to 18 months for the reality to hit us that life has forever changed. This means that a year after a divorce we can feel worse than when it first happened because the shock and numbness have finally disappeared.

Second, one loss usually brings many others. If you lose your job, you may also lose your home, your lifestyle, and close contact with coworkers and friends.

The biggest reason grief seems to last forever is we are only equipped to handle pain in small doses. Like a shaken bottle of soda and its build-up of carbonation, significant losses amass a great deal of emotional pressure within us that can only be released safely a little bit at a time. Like opening a shaken bottle of soda, if we attempt to deal with all our feelings at once, we usually end up with a big mess.

While we don't want to ignore our pain, we will, at times, need to distract ourselves. It's helpful to intentionally schedule things that bring us some relief—even if it is only briefly. Think of it like taking a break at the office. You're still working, but you step away from your desk and refresh for a few minutes. Those respites in the midst of our sorrows can give us the needed strength to "get back to work" as we deal with the realities in our lives.

Grief Is Only a Season

For a devastating loss, like the death of someone we love, it can take two to five years before we are able to rebuild and redefine what's normal. Whether it takes you months or years, give your broken heart plenty of time to heal before you become involved in another close relationship.

Although it can take a long time to grieve over our shattered dreams, sometimes grief lasts too long. We get stuck in our painful emotions, unable to move on. If it's been more than three years and you aren't showing *any hint* of forward movement, you may want to consider seeking professional help as you ask, "Is there any bitterness, resentment, or unforgiveness I'm still holding on to?" Any one of these can prevent you from rebuilding your life.

Even if you aren't stuck, be aware that just when you think the time of grief is behind you, something may trigger more sadness. The smell of a certain cologne or fragrance, the sight of a treasured photograph, or the sound of a song on the radio may remind you of what you lost. Holidays and anniversaries can also be difficult. But take heart—this is normal. It doesn't mean you're back at the beginning of the process, even though it may feel like it. There does come a day when you reach a place of acceptance and peace.

Recently a counselor told me about a woman who was going through her second divorce. Because she never grieved over the loss of her first marriage, she was especially crippled by the ending of her second one. Delayed grief, like this woman was experiencing, isn't at all unusual. Until she takes the time to grieve and let go of the past hurts and disappointments, she won't be entirely free to reach out for something new. Instead, any future heartache will bring more pain because of her unresolved emotions.

If we want healthy, vibrant relationships, we need to deal with and heal from our losses. In time we'll recognize that our pain provided a fertile environment for growth. We'll discover those times of anguish and sleepless nights gave us the opportunity to experience God's presence, power, and provision in a whole new way. We'll realize that what we thought would destroy us...God used to transform us.

Are you willing to allow God to do his redemptive work in your life? Are you willing to convert your pain to positive change?

Coaching Tip

During times of pain it's important to learn how to manage that pain as well as regularly carve out time for something that brings a few moments of relief. If you have trouble knowing what will work or tend to use unhealthy pain relievers, such as drinking too much, eating too much, or casual sex, ask, "If I had a whole day to do something wonderful and healthy, what would I choose?" Would you ride your bike or motorcycle, hike, play video games, shop, read, sleep, golf, watch TV, visit a spa, take a long bath, chill out with friends, rent a DVD or go to the movies, learn something new, entertain a few friends, fish, or travel to the beach?

Create a list of healthy stress relievers you can refer to when you're dealing with pain and not very enthusiastic about activities. When you're finished, add your own personal stress relievers to your Smart Choice Relationship Profile. When those difficult times hit, you'll already know what can refresh your soul.

Stress Relief Favorites

- Journaling my thoughts and prayers
- Walking outdoors
- Watching an uplifting or funny movie
- Dining with friends
- Going on a day trip
-
-
-
-
-

Now that we've looked at the issues that hinder our healing and growth, let's turn our attention to the attributes and habits we want to put in place to flourish in this single season of our lives. In this section we'll add the following information to our Smart Choice Relationship Profile:

- our style of connecting with God
- our community
- deal makers
- passions

Part 2

How to Choose Well

Cultivate Your Inner Life

*May your roots go down deep into the soil of God's marvelous
love; and may you be able to feel and understand, as all
God's children should, how long, how wide, how deep, and
how high His love really is; and to experience this love for
yourselves…so at last you will be filled up with God himself.*

EPHESIANS 3:17-19 TLB

I'm looking for a woman who loves Jesus more than she loves me.
I don't want to be idolized. I've already experienced the problems
that causes."

My mouth dropped open. I was interviewing a handsome, well-
educated single man at a conference. "Wow!" I said, thinking what
a wonderful guy he is. "I never heard anybody say it quite like that.
That's great."

When dating, it's easy to focus on our *outward* appearance.
Women can spend hours searching for the right outfit. Even then
we wonder, *How do I really look?* And we fret over how we should act
and what we should say. Yet, this single man made it clear what he
most wanted was a woman whose heart was centered on Christ. He
understood a healthy relationship with another person starts *within.*
He knew all too well the challenges that arise in a relationship when
our hearts are focused on something or someone besides God.

Most of us at one time or another have made a romantic relationship (or a career or a child or something else) more important than
our relationship with Christ. We've focused all our energy and attention on another person or thing instead of God. Sooner or later we
discover that those other loves can't replace the love of Christ. We

end up feeling empty and dissatisfied...like there is something missing—and there is.

In our hunger to experience closeness with others, we need to remember that the source of all loving connections is God. "God is love" (1 John 4:16). As Ruth Myers, author of *The Satisfied Heart* writes,

> We must have love. We must have *God's* love. We must have *God*, the only source of perfect, unfailing love, the only one who can fully satisfy our hearts...God's love is a love that entirely satisfies, a love that brings true happiness and inner growth. It's a love that expands and corrects our thinking, changing us both inside and out.[1]

I've found when God is my first love my heart experiences a quiet trust and peace, a feeling of having enough. When I don't focus first on him, my priorities get out of order. I put pressure on my relationships that they were never meant to bear. I get caught in the trap of expecting (and sometimes demanding) others to give me something they can't.

In order to have healthy, God-centered relationships, we first need to *let go of unrealistic expectations,* thinking one special man can be "our everything." Next, we need to *learn how* to make God a priority and trust in him. Then we need to *pay attention* to his hand in our lives, including the issues in our hearts. Practicing these things will enable us to *remain committed* even when we don't understand all that's happening.

Letting Go of Unrealistic Expectations

We may not want to let go of the illusion that a romantic partner (and later a husband) will make us whole and complete, provide us with security (inner and outer), and take away our loneliness, but if we don't, we will never experience healthy mature relationships with others.

We Expect a Romantic Relationship to Make Us Complete

Whether it is through our culture, music, parents, or recently married friends, most of us fall for the myth that when we find that special person, he or she will make us complete. Such thinking reminds me of the blockbuster movie *Jerry Maguire*.

In the film, Jerry Maguire is an aggressive sports agent whose career and personal life have crumbled. He marries Dorothy, his assistant and a single mother, because of her loyalty to him. She was one of the few people who didn't turn her back on him. After they're married, however, Dorothy realizes she loves Jerry far more than he loves her. Rather than exist in a loveless marriage, she suggests they separate.

At the very end of the film, as Jerry's career begins to look brighter, he recognizes how much Dorothy means to him. At her sister's home, in front of a divorce support group of romantically jaded women, Jerry professes his love for Dorothy including the now famous line, "You complete me."

Dorothy is totally swept off her feet (hey, it's a chick flick), despite the fact there is no proof Jerry has really changed. She tells him, "You had me at 'hello.'" This movie illustrates how Hollywood powerfully feeds the misconception that many of us cling to. We too believe we are incomplete until there is someone special in our lives. Even now, I can fall into this trap.

Recently a single girlfriend and I were attending a reunion with old friends—people who had been a key part of our world many years ago. We knew that most of those attending would be coming with their husbands or wives. While the two of us are usually quite content doing things without spouses, in this situation we felt insecure. We believed that going alone (without a man at our side) communicated that we were somehow less than our old friends.

Without saying anything to my friend, I invited a guy from my church singles group to go with me. And without telling me, my girlfriend also brought a man she had dated a couple of times.

The day after the reunion we both realized what we'd done. We'd slipped back into an old mindset. We believed we were incomplete (and somehow inferior) unless we were accompanied by men.

While many singles might *feel* more complete when we have someone to share our lives with, we need to own this misperception and understand that wholeness is only experienced in our hearts when we are filled with the love of God.

As Julie Fehr, a missionary to Africa, said, "Wholeness does not happen because I'm married or widowed or divorced, rejected or esteemed by others. That's not what makes me whole…wholeness starts in the heart…There is only one constant that will determine how you will respond to all the variables. It is your relationship with Jesus Christ."[2]

We Expect a Romantic Relationship to Provide Security

Jesus, our one constant, makes us whole and provides the only sense of true security we'll ever have in this uncertain world. However, I've heard more than one person struggling with singleness say, "But I just know if I were married, I would feel more secure." (To be honest, many of us would agree.)

In 1 Samuel 12:12 we read how the Israelites sought to find security in a human king. They wanted a leader like the other cultures around them had—one they could see, follow, and trust. This desire was not only a rejection of the Lord but showed a loss of confidence in his abilities and care. When God answered their desires and gave them King Saul, their lives were not problem-free. They simply faced different issues. When we seek someone other than God for our security, we end up disappointed. Our problems don't disappear; in fact, they're often compounded.

I could share story after story with you of how in the years I've been single God has supplied my needs in ways I never fully understood when I was married. He has used people or engineered circumstances that supported me in practical ways, and he also provided special gifts. It wasn't until I was stripped of my health, job, and marriage that I discovered my security—and yours—really doesn't lie in people, money, or wellness. It lies in God.

Twenty-five years ago I became deathly ill from complications with a bone marrow transplant. I went through a divorce. I also lost my job because I was too weak to work. Yet throughout this time I daily experienced God's protection and provision. For example, early that spring a strong March wind blew a large section of the roof off my home. The insurance company required several estimates, and every roofing contractor who submitted a bid said the same thing, "Georgia, in about two more years you will need a new roof, now at least half of it will be paid for."

Another time, years later, after I'd rebuilt my life, I longed to take my son on a cruise. However, replacing the furnace or paying for plumbing repairs seemed to always come up and take precedence. One of my coaching clients, totally unaware of my dream, bought a raffle ticket in my name for an all-expense-paid cruise for two—and I won! Kyle and I had a wonderful time on our God-given vacation arranged via Judi, who bought the ticket. I love telling the story of how God made that possible.

I'm not saying there haven't been times when I anxiously wondered how I was going to pay the property taxes or other bills. I'm not saying God's timing is always mine. But I've learned he is the only source of real security.

We Expect Someone to Take Away Loneliness

Perhaps the most popular fantasy we buy into is that romance and marriage will eliminate loneliness. Neither ever does. When I asked one friend who had recently married how loneliness in marriage differs from the loneliness she experienced when single, she replied, "When I was single and felt lonely, I relied on the Lord or would call a friend. Now that I'm married, I've come to expect my husband to take away those feelings."

She realizes how unrealistic these expectations are and how they will create real problems in her marriage if she doesn't let them go. Until I asked her that question, she hadn't realized how easily she'd slipped into the mindset of "expecting" her husband to ease her loneliness. Henri Nouwen, a late Dutch Catholic priest and writer, wrote, "Many marriages are ruined because neither partner was able to fulfill the often hidden hope that the other would take his or her loneliness away. And many celibates live with the naïve dream that in the intimacy of marriage their loneliness will be taken away."[3]

We'll deal with loneliness more in the next chapter, but right now it's essential that we remember all loving, intimate relationships begin with God. I recently heard Connie Milching speak at a women's conference about Christ being our first love. She used the phrase "first love living." I like that term because it captures where our hearts need to be focused. What is "first love living"? It means we choose to make Christ our first love, our priority, and then we cultivate a lifestyle committed to loving God with all our hearts, souls, minds, and strength (Matthew 22:37).

Connie, whose husband died at a young age while on a mission trip to Guatemala, learned firsthand the struggles of being a young widow and the value of "first love living." Today she is again married, but still she understands that God needs to be the center of her life.

Make God First

For a long time I thought making the Lord first meant I had to kiss marriage goodbye. I feared if Christ was my first love, he would never bring a man into my life. My mindset was either Jesus is *the one* or someone else would be. I'm not sure where I picked up that idea (maybe from the tradition of nuns devoting their life to Christ and never marrying).

Making God our first love doesn't disqualify us from having loving relationships. Rather, it increases the likelihood our love connection—when it happens—will be a vibrant one. Licensed clinical social worker Bob Stengel told me that the healthiest couples are those who have learned how to individually cultivate their relationship with Christ. When a couple focuses on someone bigger than themselves (God), they are both looking *first* to him to fill the empty places within their hearts rather than trying to fill their hearts with someone else.

Making the choice to stay connected with Christ means we carve out time to spend with him. It means listening to his still small voice. Jesus modeled the importance of taking time each day to connect with God the Father—our source of strength and wisdom. Jesus often slipped away to a quiet place for prayer and reflection. We need to do the same. Escaping all the distractions and demands of our lives may scare some of us. The thought of quiet time sounds too much like loneliness. In contrast Henri Nouwen wrote, "The Desert Fathers did not think of solitude as being alone, but as being alone with God. They did not think of silence as not speaking, but as listening to God. Solitude and silence are the context within which prayer is practiced."

There is no doubt we all connect with God differently. Extroverts, who are recharged by others, enjoy connecting to God in group worship, Bible studies, and small group experiences. On the other hand, introverts, whose emotional batteries are recharged by solitude, enjoy private worship as they quietly read, journal, and pray. We need to develop a good balance of both private and corporate worship. Otherwise the introverts among us become too isolated and the extroverts never slow down long enough to reflect on their lives or hear God's quiet whispers.

Over the years my private time of prayer has consistently included Scripture reading and journaling. When journaling, I'm recording my struggles and prayers. I note five things I'm thankful for that day and what I think God is communicating to me (through Scripture and his still quiet voice). Keeping a journal enables me to "listen" to God without my mind wandering off in a thousand different directions. Journaling also provides a written record of what I prayed for and how God answered each prayer. Like nothing else, the process of journaling enables me to slow down, reflect on what's going on in my life, and seek his wisdom.

Journaling might not work the same way for you. Author Gary Thomas has written about how we have different spiritual temperaments and ways of connecting and worshiping God besides being part of a community of faith. He writes,

> I read of people who found their most intimate moment with God by studying church history or theology; others were moved by singing or reading hymns; still others found their expression in dance or through a walk in the woods. All realized that a particular practice had awakened a new sense of spiritual vitality in their lives—something was touched in them that was never touched before.[4]

Regardless of our approach, in order to make smart choices, we want to seek God's counsel and wisdom on everything. All we need to do is ask: "If you need wisdom, ask our generous God, and he will give it to you" (James 1:5 NLT). In his book *My Utmost for His Highest*, Oswald Chambers says he knows "when the instructions have come from God because of their quiet persistence."[5] The question is, "Are you listening?"

Become Aware of What God Is Doing

"First love living" means paying attention or becoming aware of what God is doing and what he wants us to hear and see. It means being attuned to the condition of our hearts and asking God to illuminate anything, such as pride or bitterness that if left untended could have devastating consequences. Like King David, we should pray, "Search me, O God, and know my heart; test me and know my anxious thoughts. Point out anything in me that offends you, and lead me along the path of everlasting life" (Psalm 139:23-24 NLT).

I dated a wonderful godly man and was quickly caught up in

the excitement of meeting someone new. What fun to share with friends the stories of our incredible dates. I loved his attentiveness and all the wonderful things he said and wrote in his emails. It only took a month or so before I expected a constant diet of his affection and attention. I began seeking his approval and validation. When he didn't call or email for a couple of days I was down…way down. When he did communicate, especially something flattering or affirming, I was elated and flying high.

We all appreciate genuine compliments, but my exaggerated emotional response wasn't healthy. During my time of journaling one day, I realized what was going on. I was worshiping someone other than God. My emotional reactions were signaling that a "second love" had crept into first place in my heart. My world was revolving around my new romantic interest—what he said and did—rather than on God and what he has said and done. As soon as I noticed God's gentle prodding, I placed my budding romantic relationship in its proper perspective. As I did, I demanded less from the friendship, and the new relationship became healthier.

For all of us, whether single or married, it's so easy to slip up and get off track. The apostle Paul warns, "We must pay more careful attention, therefore, to what we have heard, so that we do not drift away" (Hebrews 2:1). When we are vigilant and consistently making time to listen to God speak, we'll be much quicker to identify signs that warn we're heading in the wrong direction. An added benefit is that we'll be less apt to find ourselves running on empty because we're being regularly refreshed with the living water of God.

In the summer, especially in the middle of a heat wave, I routinely check on my outdoor potted plants to make sure they aren't stressed from lack of water. With careful attention, I'm able to notice signs of droop or brown dry spots, alerting me the plants need water. If I notice the signs of stress early enough and take action, the plants usually recover. If I ignore them and it doesn't rain, the plants wither and eventually die.

Just as we can't expect one glass of water to quench the thirst of our potted plants all summer long, we can't expect one visit to church or one prayer here and there to give us the spiritual nourishment we need to grow and thrive spiritually. Unless we're continually replenished with God and his love, we'll soon be sporting the signs of spiritual droop and withering.

What are some general signals our souls are wilting, parched, and have brown spots? Here are some signs people have shared:

- "I know when I'm running on empty because I feel especially insecure and needy. I'm easily hurt and offended. Everything becomes a much bigger deal than it really is."

- "I can tell I'm in trouble because I start believing all those lies Satan likes to tell me—like I'm stupid or I can't do anything right. These negative thoughts compound my problems."

- "My conscience becomes callous. It doesn't bother me as much when I ignore God and do my own thing."

- "I become driven and extremely anxious."

- "When I take my eyes off God I become consumed with myself and my little world."

- "I know I'm running on empty because I'm dissatisfied with myself and my life. I start looking to others to make me happy."

- "I notice I get clingy—especially to those closest to me. I'm convinced that I need to gain their love and approval to feel worthy."

One morning I wrote in my journal, "Lord, I desperately need you today. I'm all dried up inside. Satisfy my heart as only you can." A few minutes later I headed out for a morning walk and was taken by the glorious fall colors. As I passed a wooded area, I focused on the brilliant reds, oranges, and bright yellows of the leaves. I drank in the deep-violet-blue sky. As I walked down into a valley, I marveled at how the shafts of sun so powerfully broke through thin morning fog. An hour later, when I sat down at my computer to write, I was amazed at how full I felt. God and his creation had once again nourished me in ways it's hard to explain.

Remain Committed

First love living doesn't mean we won't have times when we struggle and question what God has allowed to happen in our lives. It doesn't mean we won't have moments when we want to walk away. In John 11 is the story of Martha, Mary, and Lazarus. They were close friends of Jesus. When Lazarus became very ill, the sisters sent word to Jesus. No doubt they expected him to come quickly, but he didn't. They heard nothing. And then Lazarus died and was buried.

After the funeral Jesus finally showed up. Mary said, "Lord, if you had been here, my brother would not have died" (John 11:32). She had seen and knew the miracles Jesus had done. She knew he could heal the sick and give sight to the blind. Why hadn't he done this for her brother? He hadn't even come to the funeral!

This was the same Mary who sat at the Lord's feet and carefully listened to everything he said. This was the same Mary who made Jesus number one in her life and cultivated her relationship with him. Yet this was how her friend Jesus treated her.

Think about a close friend in your life. Suddenly someone in your family becomes deathly ill, and you call your friend to help. She doesn't return your calls. She doesn't send a card, food, or flowers. Then your loved one dies, and your friend doesn't attend the funeral. What conclusion would you come to? You would probably think, "Well, obviously she doesn't care about me. I was a fool to think we were good friends."

Mary had to be deeply hurt. She most likely failed to see what many of us miss during those times when Jesus seems to have disappeared: Jesus had a greater purpose. By waiting for four days after Lazarus' death, he planned to do something far greater than heal the sick. He was going to raise the dead!

Cultivating our inner life, our spiritual life, doesn't guarantee things will turn out the way we think or desire. Sometimes we are disappointed, hurt, and angry. Sometimes we are overcome with joy. Several years ago I felt God clearly telling me to go ahead with a large writing project. Months later, after investing weeks of time and energy, the project was rejected. I was hurt. Had I heard God correctly? I thought I had his peace to move forward. I thought I was following his will. "If I don't have a relationship with God," I told a friend, "what do I have?"

About a year later, after the project was picked up by another company—a perfect fit for me—I understood I *had* heard God correctly. I just had expected a different outcome. As author Richard Exley writes,

> If we have come often to God in the sunshine of our lives, our anxious feet will find the familiar path, even in the darkest night. Though blinded by disaster, though hounded and hindered by doubt, though confused by life which seems out of hand, we can find our way to God intuitively because going to Him has become second nature, a way of life.[6]

The more time we spend with God, the more we know we can depend on him, even though we don't immediately understand his ways or the details of our lives. Patient commitment to Christ enables us to stand firm through disappointments, betrayals, and times of stress.

I was in Southern California getting ready to leave after a hectic speaking schedule. That morning I thought of all the things I had to do—wash my hair, return several phone calls and emails, do my makeup, pack my clothes, eat breakfast, and arrive at the airport on time. I was tempted to let my time of prayer slide. But I was also aware I was close to running on empty. I took 15 minutes to sit and be with the Lord. I looked out my window, which had a lovely view of the Pacific Ocean in the distance, and breathed deeply. I listened for God's still quiet voice.

It was 6:45, and the ocean was gray. At the end of my quiet time, a mere 15 minutes later, the ocean had dramatically turned a lovely gray-blue. At that moment the Lord spoke to my heart: "Georgia, the water didn't change in 15 minutes—the light made the difference. I will make the difference in your life also—just rest in me."

Even a few minutes of connecting with God restores our hearts and souls. Cultivating our relationship with God makes a difference—all the difference in the world.

Coaching Tip

Unless we are purposeful about carving out time and space for furthering our relationship with God, it won't happen. We'll react to life, making choices we'll later regret. When we put God first, our lives don't suddenly become easier, but they do become better, enriched, and more meaningful. Any pain we experience will be used to develop our character. I love this quote by Erwin McManus in his book *The Barbarian Way:* "Jesus hasn't promised to save us from pain and suffering but from meaninglessness."[7]

Recently a divorced woman said to me, "I know I made a lot of mistakes in the past, but I also know I'll get it right the next time."

I looked her in the eyes. "Don't be so sure. Unless you are consistently cultivating your relationship with God, you might meet that guy you adore, and before you know it, you'll be so centered on him you won't even realize you've been lured away from Jesus."

In our desire for loving, intimate relationships, we need to remember that the best relationships flow out of our personal relationship with God. There is an order, and we want to make sure we put God first.

What are some of the ways you best connect with God? Have you found some of your most intimate times with him when you're listening to music or sitting on the beach? Pick your three favorite ways and note them on your Smart Choice Relationship Profile.

Also write down any signs that alert you that you're close to or running on empty. When you've become aware that you have little left, take the time to be refilled with his love. The more we experience his love, the more we flourish.

My Style of Connecting with God

- Immersing myself in his creation—walking on the beach, working in my garden, and sitting on a mountaintop.

- Reading the Bible and paying attention to the verses that jump off the page and capture my attention. What does God want me to know?

- Journaling my prayers, thoughts, and feelings, as well as what I believe God is communicating to me.

-

-

-

-

-

I'm Neglecting My Relationship with God When...

- I'm extremely anxious.
- I focus on the negative.
- I lose sight of the bigger picture—God's plans and purposes.

-

-

-

-

-

Build a Supportive Community

If one falls down, his friend can help him up.
But pity the man who falls and has no one
to help him up!

ECCLESIASTES 4:10-11

One of the challenges of being single is the mistaken belief that we need to go it alone. God created us to be in relationship with him, but also with others. We need people with whom to share our lives. Living in isolation is downright dangerous. A supportive social network is vital for helping us establish and maintain healthy lives. King Solomon spoke of the power of being connected with others: "A person standing alone can be attacked and defeated, but two can stand back-to-back and conquer. Three are even better, for a triple-braided cord is not easily broken" (Ecclesiastes 4:12 NLT).

In our society, deep and meaningful connections are dwindling. Twenty-five percent of Americans today report having no one in whom to confide compared with only ten percent two decades ago.[1] With our iPads, laptops, TVs, and other electronics, we tune out those around us. We often focus on our careers, leaving little time and energy for social interactions. And we sometimes give the relationships we do have superficial attention because we connect by texting, email, or talking on our phones while driving or shopping. This tendency is eliminating the face-to-face connections that contribute to deep relationships essential for our emotional well-being. The more connected we are technologically, the less connected we are socially.

Another trend gaining momentum is the attitude that total independence is a good thing. Maybe this belief evolved from disappointed children growing up in fractured families. Or maybe it grew out of our society's increasing orientation to self. Regardless of the reason, there seems to be the mindset that we're not going to be emotionally vulnerable to or dependent on or constricted by anyone else. Columnist David Brooks says young people of today "romanticize independence" while being "desperate for companionship."[2]

There is nothing romantic about independence. Going it alone makes us vulnerable and needy. Without close friends and a supportive social circle we not only become easy targets for predatory people, but we also miss out on opportunities for growth and maturity. As Eugene Peterson writes, "I am not myself by myself. Community, not the highly vaunted individualism of our culture, is the setting in which Christ is at play."[3]

"But I want a family of my own—not a community," one single woman told me. "Anything else sounds like a booby prize." Many of us yearn for our own families, but a family doesn't always have to mean the traditional husband, wife, and children. We can create a special family with our friends, neighbors, coworkers, and fellow church members, as well as with relatives.

When discussing the value of a social network, I realize most of us have a few people in our community who might impact us in negative ways. If possible, we want to distance ourselves from these people and recognize the potentially toxic impact they have on our emotional and physical well-being. In *Social Intelligence,* Daniel Goleman discusses how emotions are contagious ("We can catch a whiff of emotions from something as fleeting as a glimpse of a smile or frown"[4]), and when we're involved in difficult relationships our stress hormones increase, which in turn compromises our immune systems. That said, a *healthy* social network is crucial for singles because it...

- makes us less vulnerable to loneliness

- creates an environment for growth
- encourages us during the stressful times

Countering Loneliness

Diet experts understand that total deprivation leads to binge-ing. When we're famished, we desperately reach for anything, usu-ally junk food, to satisfy our hunger. In the same way, when we lack healthy interactions we will try to satisfy our cravings for social con-nection with anybody close by, which could include people who aren't good for us.

God designed us for relationships. Loneliness is like a gauge on a vehicle dashboard. It alerts us to the fact we're running low on relation-ship fuel and need to connect with others. And like a fuel-driven car, we constantly need to fill up our tanks or we'll be depleted. Loneliness can creep into our lives when we least expect it. So how can we handle it? Being intentional about building and maintaining a social circle will help to meet our ongoing needs for companionship.

Ally's job requires a great deal of travel. She can spend months in a city while working on a large project. At one point she "lived" in Chicago, where she dated Justin for about six months. Once her assignment in Chicago ended, so did their relationship. A year later Ally happened to return to Chicago for a different assignment. She had no sooner arrived at the airport and boarded the shuttle to her hotel when the familiar sights and sounds bombarded her. She missed Justin, but he was now engaged.

By the time she reached her hotel and unpacked her suitcases, she knew she had to do something. She considered heading to the bar to find companionship and a drink or drowning herself in a romance novel, but she knew the best choice was to pray and then phone a close friend. When one of her friends didn't answer, she tried two others, each time leaving a message that she was having a rough day. About an hour later a friend returned her call.

Ally told me later, "Just knowing there were people who cared about me—that I wasn't all alone in the world—made the awful ache easier to handle."

We need at least one person in our lives with whom we can share our honest feelings, such as, "My life stinks right now." We need someone safe—someone who keeps our confidences, cares about our well-being, and who will be available even when it's not convenient. And don't wait for people to reach out to you. Be the kind of friend you seek. Begin investing in the lives of others. Deep, meaningful connections take time, so be patient. Psychology professor John Gottman writes, "Complex, fulfilling relationships don't suddenly appear in our lives fully formed. Rather, they develop one encounter at a time."[5] One encounter added to another over time has the potential to give friendship the depth needed to make it very special and supportive.

While close friends are crucial, it's important that we are also willing to widen our social circle. My inner social circle includes a few close friends—some who are married and some who are single, some who live several miles from me and some who live thousands of miles away. When I was first divorced, I didn't have any close *single* friends. I now understand how singles provide a unique perspective. And now that I'm single again, they provide a support my married friends don't. If I say, "I hate not having someone special during the Christmas season," singles know exactly what that feels like.

On the other hand, my married friends help me balance my life by giving me their viewpoints and the opportunity to enjoy couples' events without a partner. Whether they realize it or not they also provide me with a gentle reminder, every now and then, that being married has its problems too.

My social network is also made up of my biological family, which includes my son and mother, as well as my extended family, such as aunts and cousins. Then I have my close spiritual friend—a special woman who helps me to pay attention to God's hand in my life. I'm also part of a writer's group that has met for years and truly has become family. My community includes relationships within my church and the singles group there. Whether we pray together or laugh together, these people support me in numerous ways.

Establishing Community

You can begin building your social network or family by joining a group that is already established. Look for people who share your interests and values. For years my church singles group was not only a wonderful spiritual community, but also a great social network. Every summer we spent a week at the ocean, vacationing in a dormitory setting. And year after year I experienced how much this community became family to me. Each day on our beach trip we were free to do whatever we enjoyed by ourselves or join in with others. There were usually small groups playing board games, sitting on the beach, biking, going out to eat, and taking ocean excursions. Everyone felt included—singles with no children as well as single parents with their children.

What touched me the most were the little encounters that took place naturally. I saw one of the older teenage girls teach one of the younger girls, who lived with her single father, how to do her makeup. I overheard one seven-year-old declare to one of the older girls after a shopping trip, "You'll be a great mommy someday." I watched some of the single men do fatherly activities (biking or throwing footballs) with boys who had no dads actively involved in their lives. One year a five-year-old created a sense of family by drawing little pictures on tablet paper and tucking them under everyone's door at night.

Whether it was the bonding times in the bathroom (one big bathroom for each sex with many showers, sinks, and toilets) each morning and evening or an evening of karaoke, we shared priceless moments on our inexpensive family vacation.

Last summer I asked Steve, one of the guys on the beach trip, to describe what his relationship with one of his friends from our group meant to him. Steve said, "I couldn't tell you in two days how much it has enriched my life."

God does set the lonely in families, just like Psalm 68:6 says—
it's just not always the family we imagine.

Creating a Growth Environment

As we widen our social circle and get to know more people, we'll
discover there are certain folks who remain acquaintances and others with whom we develop stronger and deeper relationships. The
latter inspire us to grow and become better people. These friends
accept us as we are while encouraging us to grow. They also sometimes tell us what we need to hear. Close friends challenge us by
asking tough questions, and they help us see ourselves and our problems differently.

They accept us as we are.

Linda, one of my close friends, has given me grace when I didn't
deserve it and patiently listened to my dating sagas. She knows
nearly everything about me, yet she loves and accepts me as I am.
But it's taken years to develop this type of connection. Over time, as
Linda and I slowly revealed parts of ourselves we didn't want others
to know, we learned we can trust one another. Being real with someone is risky so we have a tendency to keep parts of ourselves hidden
because we believe if people knew our junk they wouldn't like us.
The beauty is when they do know who we really are and they still
accept us and love us, it gives us the freedom to be ourselves. This
acceptance inspires us and gives us the confidence to change and
grow. The more connected we feel toward someone, the more we
will allow them to share in the hard stuff about ourselves so we can
hear their views and mature.

They tell us what we need to hear.

One of my friends joined an Internet dating site. When she
found someone she enjoyed being with (after a couple of dates),
she invited a few of her godly friends into the process. "Godly" is
the key word. Listening to the advice of those who don't share our

values usually creates more problems for us. There is always someone who will tell us what we want to hear, which may or may not be what we *need* to hear.

In my friend's case, she decided to share with us snippets of emails and conversations from her new date. She invited those of us who knew her best to give honest feedback about him and their relationship. She'd learned from experience that Internet dating can create a false sense of intimacy with someone we only know in one dimension. She understood that unless we see people on a regular basis, we don't get a true sense of how they relate to "real" people and how they live their lives.

When one of us pointed out that it appeared the hours and hours the two of them were spending on the phone might be creating a deeper connection before they really had a chance to know each other, my friend willingly cut back on the amount of time they chatted on the phone so they'd create more face-to-face opportunities.

In the chapters on blind spots we discussed how the opinions of those we trust can help us avoid fatal attractions. However, the suggestions of others are only valuable to the degree we are willing to be vulnerable and real. If my friend who was online dating had failed to share with us that her instincts said something wasn't quite right about this man, we might have missed alerting her to what may be a real red flag. If she only shared the positive parts of their interactions, the things she really wanted us to hear, our opinions wouldn't have been valid or accurate.

It is equally important when inviting people to give us feedback that we are receptive and open to their suggestions. If we ask people to be honest, and then we lash out or snub them when their opinions are not what we want to hear, they will stop sharing the truth. They'll learn that we don't mean it when we ask for advice.

In order to grow we have to tolerate a certain amount of discomfort in our closest relationships. Inviting people to challenge us and ask us the tough questions can be uncomfortable…and humbling.

Obviously we only want to do this with people who will give us the truth with love, integrity, and compassion.

A good indicator of how we will do in a marital relationship is how well we relate to others in our current connections. Successful marriages don't *begin* on the wedding day. We need to be aware of and seek feedback about how our choices, words, and actions affect others. As author and psychologist Henry Cloud says, "We're entitled to know the truth about ourselves and the damage we cause to each other."[6]

How would those closest to you describe their relationship with you? Is there anything they find particularly annoying or bothersome? Here are a few questions to ponder or consider asking someone.

Do those closest to you find you...

- encouraging or critical
- emotionally present or distant and distracted
- other-centered or self-centered
- authentic and real or hiding behind a false image
- caring of them or clueless to what they're experiencing
- listening intently or constantly interrupting
- willing to admit when you're wrong or never apologizing
- dependable and responsible or someone they can't count on

Mutual caring and commitment in our relationships makes a real difference in life quality. If feedback from someone reveals you need to strengthen the skill of listening, be willing to work on it to enhance your friendships...and life in general.

Many times we can figure out what we need to work on by simply paying attention to our interactions. How many of us have caught ourselves not focusing on a conversation so the other person clams up? You feel bad. An opportunity for deep sharing has been missed, and you disappointed your friend. When this happens, apologize and try again.

Practice being more focused on others. Actively listen and note how people are talking. Often you'll discover a clue that can lead to a deeper conversation: "You sounded tired at the staff meeting yesterday. How are you doing?"

Maturity and growth in our relationships is marked by being a good friend rather than being obsessed with whether or not we have good friends. Biblically we are encouraged to love others, *to give of ourselves.* "Observe how Christ loved us. His love was not cautious but extravagant. He didn't love in order to get something from us but to give everything of himself to us. Love like that" (Ephesians 5:2 MSG). We don't love to get; we love to give.

Encourage Each Other

For singles, there can be plenty of drama and heartache, but the worst thing we can do is suffer silently. McKenzie was swept off her feet by a man at work who showered her with gifts, lovely dinners, and constant attention. Then, for no apparent reason, she heard nothing from him. The few times their paths crossed he ignored her and looked in the opposite direction. "For two weeks I came home from work and just sat in my dark apartment thinking what a neurotic mess I am. I was convinced that *everyone,* including this latest guy, thinks I'm a real loser." Finally she poured out her heart to a dear friend. "Within minutes she had me laughing. She encouraged me by reminding me of the struggles I'd survived in the past. She told me, 'Hey, we all have moments when we feel like we're crazy or are sure there is something horribly wrong with us,'" McKenzie shared.

What meant the most to McKenzie was when her friend said,

"You've been here for me oodles of time. Now it's my turn to be here for you. I don't want you to stew in all that negative thinking. Call me anytime—even if it's three in the morning."

Like McKenzie, we all need people to be safety nets for us during stressful times—people who will encourage us when we are discouraged or so overwhelmed we can't deal with the burden we're carrying. We need people who will pray with us and listen to our stories without judging or trying to fix us.

No one heals from emotional wounds alone. We need people to cheer us on when we doubt ourselves, someone who will point us to God and won't let us give up even when we feel hopeless.

As we cultivate our friendships and widen our social circles, we're not only investing in others as we learn more about ourselves, but we're developing the skills necessary for developing and maintaining healthy relationships. Don't sit on the sidelines. Intentionally build a social network and remember that relationships aren't always about convenience. And who knows, maybe one day you'll find yourself so blessed by your social network that you'll feel like Sasha, a never-married woman who said, "Relationships do take work, but I had no idea that my life could be so rich and full *without* a husband and children."

Coaching Tip

The benefit of intentionally cultivating our social networks means we will no longer be starving for healthy relationships. It means we will create an environment in which we can thrive and grow and help others do the same.

Take a few moments to identify the people who make up your current community. Who are your closest friends? Do you have people who will accept you as you are and show you God's grace? Do you have a friend you can call when your life gets messy? Do you have someone who will speak the truth to you in love, someone who will encourage you when you're discouraged, someone who will listen closely when you need to talk? And are you willing to do this for others?

Evaluate the kinds of relationships you have and then record them in your Smart Choice Relationship Profile. Be willing to eliminate anything in your life taking the place of real relationships, such as characters on your favorite TV show.

Make the time to invest in the lives of others and develop a strong social network. If no one is including you right now, reach out to those you would like to get to know better. One single woman recently formed a group with seven other singles. One Friday night a month they go to a new restaurant in town. Why not start your own group?

List those who are in your social network and your closest support system. For example, I could list my biological family, church family, close friends, the singles group at church, friends from high school, roommates from college, writing and speaking friends, my brother, my parents, and my best friend.

My Social Network

-

-

-

-

-

My Closest Support

-

-

-

-

-

-

Choose Character over Chemistry

Follow your heart without losing your mind.[1]

JOHN VAN EPP

When a chick flick ends with the hero and heroine happily entwined, women sigh with longing. But is that romantic "in love" feeling really *the* ultimate?

"The experience of falling in love is invariably temporary," wrote psychiatrist Scott Peck in *The Road Less Traveled*.

> No matter whom we fall in love with, we sooner or later fall out of love if the relationship continues long enough. This is not to say that we invariably cease loving the person with whom we fell in love. But it is to say that the feeling of ecstatic lovingness that characterizes the experience of falling in love always passes. The honeymoon always ends. The bloom of romance always fades.[2]

Admittedly most women are romanced by the idea of romance. Falling in love is intoxicating. We love being swept off our feet. And I'm not suggesting we ignore those passionate feelings; however, once we understand these elated emotions are *temporary*, we are far less likely to be caught up in the craziness of romantic fantasies. Emotional and spiritual maturity means we experience the joy of the moment (that emotional high), appreciate romance and love, but don't buy into the myth that euphoric feelings will have the same intensity forever.

Knowing the fireworks calm down, how can we best approach dating to develop meaningful relationships that will last? Relationship expert John Van Epp states that what is essential for healthy relationships is to balance head knowledge with heart knowledge: "Too often people act on the belief that being in love entitles them to stop taking in and analyzing information about their partners. The assumption is that love itself will take care of all that is to come." I think most of us know more than one failed relationship where love didn't simply take care of itself.

Smart choices are based on how we feel (heart) and what we know to be true (head). However, there is also a spiritual dimension important for good decision making. We make the wisest choices in dating when we keep our heads and hearts in balance while staying tuned to the wisdom of God. An easy way to remember this approach is to think of 3 H's—Heart, Head, and Holy Spirit. In other words, listen to your heart, use your head, and obey the Holy Spirit.

Listen to Your Heart

When it comes to paying attention to matters of the heart, be aware that most of us tend to drift toward one of two extremes— we either blindly open our hearts and ourselves for anyone or we keep a protective wall around ourselves that we won't take down for anyone.

There is a scene in the movie *Hitch* that vividly portrays these two approaches. Will Smith, who plays Alex Hitchens (Hitch), is known as the "date doctor" and considered one of New York City's best dating coaches. However, given the fact that Hitch helps men gain and keep the attention of the women of their dreams, Hitch finds it necessary to be discreet about who his clients are. Only his clients know that Hitch is *the* dating doctor. Gossip columnist Sara (Eva Mendes) discovers that Hitch is the "date doctor" and plasters his picture on the front page of the newspaper, along with a photograph of one of his clients—Albert (Kevin James) and a date. Not only does this shatter Hitch's career, but it also destroys Albert's love life.

Shortly after this humiliating exposure, Hitch is in his upscale apartment packing up his belongings when Albert dejectedly walks in and asks Hitch to fix things so he can get back with the woman he loves.

"I got nothing, Albert," Hitch says and then suggests they go out for the evening.

Albert isn't interested. "Honestly," he says, "I never knew I could feel like this. I swear I'm going out of my mind. I wanna throw myself off of every building in New York. I see a cab and I wanna dive in front of it because then I'll stop thinking about her."

"Look, you will. Just give it time."

"That's just it! I don't want to. I've waited my whole life to feel this miserable. If this is the only way I can stay connected with her, then this is who I have to be."

Then with all the passion of someone who has vowed never to be hurt again, Hitch retorts, "No, you don't! You can change; you can adapt. You can make it so you don't ever have to feel like this ever again."

Which one of these two men can you best relate to? Do you tend to get so caught up in those wild and wonderful feelings that you want to jump in front of a cab when the relationship ends? Or do you tend to be cautious, maybe to the point of never taking risks so you won't be vulnerable ever again to the pain of a broken heart?

We need to allow ourselves to connect emotionally with others without building walls or running away. It's equally imperative that we "guard our hearts" and use our heads, knowing that the passionate "in love" feeling is mostly temporary and can mislead us into thinking every new person is "the one."

Use Your Head

Maybe we can't always pick the person with whom we experience "sparks" of attraction, but we can *choose* what we do about those sparks. We aren't powerless over these attractions. Scott Peck states that although it may involve self-discipline, "We can choose how to respond to the experience of falling in love."[3]

Imagine you have two fires. One is started by lighting a match near vapors of natural gas. There's an explosion and a fire quickly flares up. The blaze only lasts for a few minutes before it dies. In contrast, the second fire starts by lighting a few pieces of kindling. It smolders quietly and then turns into a slow-burning fire that intensifies over time. This kind of blaze can burn for years. In Centralia, Pennsylvania, a fire has been burning since 1962. It continues today because it is fueled by underground veins of coal. If fire is a metaphor for your love life, which type of fire would you prefer: a quick-burning blaze that might explode in your face and die quickly or the smoldering, slow-burning one that lasts?

Using our heads means we don't intentionally add an accelerant or stoke the love fire too quickly by being, for example, sexually intimate. Using our heads means we realize that just as some chemicals mixed together are very reactive, there are certain dating combinations that are highly flammable and can create out-of-control wildfires. Examples of dangerous or out-of control relationships include dating someone who has an addiction, someone who has just broken up with another person, and someone who is terrified of being alone and is desperate for any relationship.

Not only do we want to protect ourselves from these unhealthy relationships, but using our heads also means if the chemistry is there and it *appears* to be a healthy relationship, we intentionally "contain the fire" until we consider these four things: character, compatibility, communication, and commitment.

Consider Character

By character, I'm referring to the distinctive qualities of people that reveal important information about who they really are. As Dwight L. Moody said, "Character is what you are in the dark." [4] Character is the way someone behaves even when there is no one around to impress or be accountable to.

Sometimes, as mentioned earlier, the best way to judge character is not only to evaluate how people treat you, but also observe how they treat others, especially those in their families or in service positions, including servers, door attendants, and waste haulers. Are they kind? Gentle? Honest? Respectful?

One single woman dated a man who had the reputation of being so caring of others that he once made a business decision that financially hurt him but protected his employees. During the years they dated she witnessed this same compassion and concern for others in numerous situations. Another man who was single again told me the character traits he most appreciated in the woman he was seeing were that she was adaptable, stable, and could be trusted to keep her word. In both these cases, behavior indicated markers of people worthy of their time and affection.

Have you stopped to consider or write down the character traits you most value? Do you like people who are positive about life and grateful for what others do for them? Do you want someone who is committed to putting Christ first? If you don't have a clear picture of which qualities are most important to you, how will you know if you are close to your desired goal?

Peruse this list of character traits. Consider which ones are important to you in a potential partner. Pick your top three and add them to your Smart Choice Relationship Profile.

I want someone who is…

accepting	affectionate	authentic
career-minded	committed	compassionate
confident	cooperative	empathetic
faithful	family-minded	flexible
friendly	fun	funny
generous	gentle	happy
hardworking	healthy	honest

honorable	humble	joyful
just	kind	knowledgeable
mannerly	organized	patient
peaceful	powerful	protective
reliable	responsible	sensitive
spiritual	teachable	trustworthy
truthful	unflappable	wise

Consider Compatibility

Compatibility refers to more than the fact that you both are Christians or that you both love to ski and dance. We want to consider many areas—emotional, social, intellectual, physical, and spiritual. As my friend Gayle Roper has reminded me more than once, it's a cluster of things that makes you compatible:

> It isn't enough to have that zing of physical attraction and be comfortable with someone. It isn't enough to know they are nice and you enjoy being with them. It isn't enough that the person be a committed Christian, though that's imperative. All these things are important, but what's most essential is the combination of all these things. Do you have the mental and spiritual connection with the physical attraction and common interests? It's all these things put together that creates a great relationship.

I didn't always pay close attention to the importance of how interests worked together. Several years ago I invited the man I was seriously dating to have dinner with two of my friends visiting from out of town. It was important to me that they meet him before I became even more emotionally attached.

One of the women brought along a deck of core value cards.

Someone in her family used them in a group exercise at work, and she thought it would be fun and helpful. Each card contained a word, such as beauty, fun, knowledge, and wisdom. The idea was to read through the stack of cards and pick the ten cards that best represent your core values. Then you were to narrow the list down to your five most important ones.

That night my five choices were:

- faith
- family
- integrity
- excellence
- beauty

The man I was dating chose:

- fun
- food
- knowledge
- trust
- family

I looked at his list. I reviewed my list. Then I had one of those *Aha!* experiences. Although we both had family on our top five, I knew that at our ages (over 45), he meant *his* family (daughter, grandchildren, parents, siblings) and, likewise, I meant my son, my mother, and my aunt. The bigger problem was that the most important value to me (faith) wasn't even in his top five. Although I like to have fun and eat, food isn't on my top 20 list.

I'm not suggesting that you and the person you date need to have identical lists because that's not necessary. Sometimes it can be enlightening to hear his or her reasoning as to why the values were chosen. For example, food may be picked because it symbolizes loving interactions with family and friends. If you're considering a long-term relationship, don't ignore your differing top core values or pretend the choices aren't important enough to be considered further.

I love the phrase Billy Graham and his wife used to describe their relationship. They were "happily incompatible." They respected one another's differences as well as enjoyed their similarities and shared visions. It was the "shared vision" that my friend and I lacked. I failed to realize this truth because I'd simply been focused on the fact we had good chemistry and he was a Christian.

Please take some time to develop your own list of core values. (Visit the free resources page at www.GeorgiaShaffer.com for a free downloadable PDF of value cards you can print out.) You want to be aware of your core values *before* getting into a relationship. That way when you become seriously involved with someone, you'll be able to determine how compatible the two of you really are. When one woman compared her core values with the guy she was dating, she told me, "Georgia, I realized the two of us were not only not on the same page, we weren't even in the same book."

Consider Communication

Communication is essential for deep connections. Perhaps the most profound research on the communication of couples has been by psychologist and relationship expert John Gottman. With 94 percent accuracy, he predicted which couples in the study would be divorced in three years. Those who were exceptionally critical of their partners, the kind of criticism that is filled with contempt, were most likely to destroy their relationship.[5]

Gottman says that being emotionally open is key to *building* close connections. Emotional openness means we feel safe and are willing to express our inner thoughts and feelings with people so they feel connected to us. For example, Michelle was the kind of person who found it difficult to be vulnerable and tell someone she missed them. For her to share with the man she was dating that she'd missed seeing him over the past weekend because of their busy schedules was a big step for her.

Gottman also writes that we all long for evidence that others really care about what we are feeling.[6] When people share their real emotions, it's important to validate them in a way that lets them know they are accepted by us. That kind of communication shows we really care. If the guy you're dating calls to say he had a rough day and needs to talk, telling him you're too busy right now won't make him feel very special. If you can stop what you're doing, listen intently, and express your concern, a deeper emotional connection may be established between the two of you.

Is your romantic interest willing to talk about his real emotions? When you share yours, does your date validate and communicate that he gets what you're sharing? How attuned are you to one another? Can you both be authentic and real and respectful when discussing an issue? Do you both have the freedom to bring up a problem and sometimes disagree? Can you both be vulnerable and fully present to each other? Good communication facilitates connection and feelings of security, safety, and warmth.

Consider Commitment

Kendall has gone out with Chris for almost six months. They spent Christmas, New Year's, and Valentine's Day together. One evening she asked, "How would you define our relationship?"

"I would say we are friends…good friends."

"Really?" Kendall was surprised and disappointed. She and many of her friends would have said she and Chris were dating…even seriously dating. Kendall felt Chris had come to expect a level of emotional intimacy and investment of time that was beyond ordinary friendship. She wondered, *Is Chris able or willing to make a real commitment to me, even if it's just saying we're officially dating?*

There is no doubt that the ability to commit is related to a person's character. Does he do what he promises to do? Does she keep her word? Does he understand obligation? Does she recognize the constraints and responsibilities that come with making promises?

Let's address commitment in terms of a dating relationship because that frequently comes up in situations like Kendall's and in conversations with my single friends. I hear people say, "He's a commitment-phobe." "I think he's committed to being uncommitted." "He wants to live together but won't make the commitment to get married."

Maybe you're dating someone who is honest about the struggles in life, and you can trust him to do what he says he will do. You're compatible spiritually, emotionally, and mentally. You can talk about the deeper issues even when they are difficult to say and even harder to hear. But he won't commit to a long-term relationship for some reason...

- Perhaps he wants to keep his options open and explore other possibilities (not that he's verbalized this).

- Maybe he's driven by fear of failure and feels safe knowing he can always end the relationship if he sees trouble on the horizon.

- Perhaps he doesn't trust his ability to choose well because of poor choices he's made in the past.

- Perhaps he sees relationships in light of convenience rather than commitment.

- Maybe he has a history of divorce in his family and wants to live together to avoid the upheaval and pain divorce can bring (as if it's not painful to break up with someone you're living with!).

Regardless of the reason, before you decide to move forward with someone, it's important to determine whether this person has the ability or willingness to make a long-term commitment. Will he persevere when the relationship becomes uncomfortable or painful? Can he look you in the eye and say, "I'm in this for the long haul"? If your dating relationship moves toward marriage, can you trust him to stay in the marriage when difficulties arise? When your health fails? When finances are tight? When jobs are lost?

If the person you're seriously dating hasn't demonstrated the ability to be committed, or you don't have the confidence that he will be there for you when things get tough, it's time to assess whether or not this is the kind of relationship you're looking for.

Obeying the Holy Spirit

While we want to be in touch with our feelings (our hearts), and we want to use our heads, most importantly we need to seek the wisdom and peace of God through prayer and Scripture. God isn't going to send us out into the dating world alone. He promises, "I will guide you along the best pathway for your life. I will advise you and watch over you" (Psalm 32:8 NLT). All we need to do is ask and then follow the path he directs us to.

If you aren't sure what to do, *wait* until you have God's peace. I especially like what Oswald Chambers says: "I know when the instructions have come from God because of their quiet persistence."[7] It's God's consistent, gentle taps on our shoulders that we don't want to ignore. We never want to walk away from God and his perfect love, especially for someone else's imperfect love.

One of my friends who is now married told me that years ago she thought God wanted her to marry a missionary or a pastor, but the man she was dating had no such intent. He seemed right in almost every other way, so she was confused. What was God's will? As they continued dating, she prayed many prayers asking for guidance, for a sign. All of God's answers continued pointing her in the same direction: marriage to this man. The day before he proposed, she took a four-hour drive alone, during which she prayed, "God, if you don't want me to marry him, please stop me." God didn't. That couple has now been happily married for more than 25 years. Today they talk about possibly doing missionary or volunteer work when they retire. Because my friend followed God's leading and married this man, she was able to see how God can work in a person's heart and change dreams and plans.

One of the common myths about love is if we don't have that chemistry that knocks us off our feet or it isn't "love at first sight," it really isn't the kind of love that will last. The reality about the initial euphoric feeling is that it's *not* love. If you don't know someone, "you can only fall in love with the idea of that type of person, not the actual person himself. It takes seasons of life, intimate moments, difficult obstacles, and unwavering faith to really fall in love with someone."[8]

In order to make intelligent love choices, be patient and carefully consider the three H's—Heart, Head, and Holy Spirit, giving the latter the most weight. The "in love" feeling may be temporary, but meaningful, long-lasting relationships are not.

Coaching Tip

We want to be clear on what we want in our special someones so we don't accept less. What kind of person are you seeking? What character qualities are most important to you? What are your core values? Your interests?

We may get out of balance on the physical side, wanting to date someone who is especially attractive physically. On the other hand, we may settle for any relationship, particularly if we perceive it offers a sense of security. So take the time to consider all the different aspects and traits and then record your list of "deal-makers"—what matters most to you...what you absolutely have to have in a partner.

Maybe you won't find someone with everything on your list, but at least you'll know what you're shooting for. Dr. Phil McGraw says we're wasting our time if we are looking for the perfect match. He writes, "Look for the guy who is free of the deal breakers and has 80 percent of what you do want in a partner. The other 20 percent you can grow. If the guy has 80 percent of what you want and potential to grow the extra 20 percent, you need to bag that boy up because he is good to go. Do not walk past him while you're looking for Mr. 100 Percent."[9] Although Dr. Phil may say the guy's good to go, don't forget to wait for God to give you the green light.

For most of us the problem is we'll never know if we've found 80 percent of what's most important to us until we make our list. Do it now *before* your brain is short-circuited by that passionate "in love" feeling.

One friend has clarified her deal-makers and said I could share them with you: committed to Christ, humble, very intelligent, well spoken, easy on the eyes. Maybe you would also choose a guy with integrity, a generous spirit, a heart to serve others, and a passion to grow.

Once you've identified your deal-makers, write them down and transfer them to your Smart Choice Relationship Profile.

Top Five Deal-Makers

-

-

-

-

-

Manage the Ongoing Challenges

The rung of a ladder was never meant to rest
upon, but only to hold a man's foot long enough to
enable him to put the other somewhat higher.[1]

THOMAS HENRY HUXLEY

I was nestled in bed doing one of my favorite things—reading. The words didn't register in my mind as much as they resonated in my soul. With tears filling my eyes, I realized Ronald Rolheiser had identified some of the rumbling feelings stuck deep inside of me. He expressed those emotions and thoughts I was barely aware of. Rolheiser, in *Forgotten Among the Lilies,* wrote:

> Unlike married persons and consecrated religious [priests and nuns], few single persons feel they have positively chosen their state of life. They feel victimized into it. Few single persons feel relaxed, easeful and accepting of their lot.
>
> The feeling instead is always that this must be temporary. Rarely can a young single person project his or her future acceptingly to the end and see him or herself growing old and dying single and happy. Invariably the feeling is this: Something has to happen to change this! I do not choose this! I cannot see myself for the rest of my life like this![2]

When I read those words, I realized I could visualize myself dying single or dying happy, but not dying happy and single. To be happy and single was not a combination I *ever* imagined.

What was especially interesting about this new revelation was that during my bone marrow transplant almost 25 years ago, I did almost die, and the last thing on my mind was whether or not I was dying single and happy. I was much too sick to be concerned about my marital status or emotional state. I was more concerned about surviving and living to see my then ten-year-old son grow up.

In the years since the transplant, I have (for the most part) experienced real peace and joy without a spouse. The obvious question I need to ask is why couldn't I see myself dying single and happy? What about that scenario was I unwilling to accept? And face it, even if I was married today, there's no guarantee I wouldn't die single or sad.

As I read Rolheiser's book I became aware of one more issue of singleness I needed to explore. Was I willing to accept my current marital status for the rest of my life? Would I accept and enjoy the gift of the single life I had been given and be the person God created me to be, today and in the future? Or would I feel sorry for myself and attempt to manipulate my circumstances? Would I choose to settle for any man who might be less than God's best just to feel secure in some false way? Or was I going to really trust God?

No matter where we are in our journeys of singleness, and no matter how emotionally and spiritually healthy we might be, we *will* have times when we are restless, dissatisfied, and challenged by our single status. There will be times when we don't like where we are or where we appear to be heading. That's normal; that's life. The issue isn't that we struggle with our singleness as much as what we do with our attitudes and feelings. Looking for someone to make us happy or ignoring our feelings and fears about the challenges that pop up along the way isn't going to give us the results we want. But when we're willing to tackle our inner conflicts, we often discover that the change needed is in our hearts and in the way we look at our situation.

For example, one young man considered becoming a priest, but he didn't like the idea of dying alone. He wanted to die like his father did—in the arms of his wife. He said, "One day I was meditating on Christ's life and it struck me powerfully that He died alone, loved…but in nobody's arms. He was really alone [in one way], though he was powerfully linked to everyone in a different way. It struck me that this could also be a good way to die!"

The thought of dying alone is only one of the challenges we wrestle with as singles. There are also issues dealing with holidays, breaking up, risking again, needing touch, and desiring physical intimacy. By being proactive and intentionally addressing these issues, we can reduce our vulnerability to making poor choices.

The Challenge of Holidays

Let's face it—holidays can be the pits. Some of them, such as Christmas and Valentine's Day, are especially difficult when we don't usually experience Hallmark moments. My friend Olivia told me that Christmas and New Year's Eve are her toughest holidays. She said, "Every year I go to my sister's for Christmas dinner, and every year I'm the only one there who isn't married. I join in their festivities and try to have fun, but I always end up feeling like the proverbial fifth wheel." This year Olivia planned ahead and traveled to a resort over Christmas. She said, "It was the best Christmas I've had in years."

Christmas Eve is the time of year most likely to trip me up. Since I know it can be difficult, I make plans to attend church with my son and family or to serve as a greeter during the evening service.

"I struggle with Valentine's Day," another single said. "If I'm not dating anyone, I feel so less than desirable. That's when I'm especially starved for affection."

Regardless of the holiday you struggle with, make the decision not to sit at home alone. Remind yourself that this particular day doesn't have to be about having a significant other in your life. Do something you enjoy and invite those who have no plans to join you. My friend Deb and I still talk about the Valentine's Day when we had dinner at an elegant restaurant and brought long stem roses for each other. Another single gal who annually coordinates a

Valentine's Day dinner and movie for herself and four friends said, "I've had so much more fun with my girlfriends on Valentine's Day then I ever did when I was dating or married."

You may not have a choice as to whether or not you're single during the holidays, but you can make a choice on how you spend those days.

The Challenge of Breaking Up

Although we discussed grieving over a broken relationship in chapter 7, there are many other issues surrounding this topic. One of the biggest challenges is our unwillingness to break up with someone even when we know the relationship is not what God wants. And often we hang on even when we're aware the relationship isn't working. Maybe we're caught up in an abusive relationship, and it's difficult or dangerous to break up. In this case, we need to tread cautiously, seek professional help, and have a support system in place. Sometimes we continue the relationship because it's comfortable. Lauren said, "I knew it was time to end things with my boyfriend but I thought, *What am I going to do on Friday nights?*"

We also hesitate to end a relationship because there is something about not having *any possibilities*—no one we are even slightly interested in or who is interested in us—that can leave us feeling hopeless about the future and make it difficult to remember our true identity lies in God.

When I was having problems ending a relationship that was going nowhere, a friend said, "Georgia, how will you have space for someone new to come into your life if you haven't let go of this relationship?" Call it coincidence, but I took her advice and a month after I made a clean break and ended the relationship, I started dating someone else who hadn't been on the radar a month earlier.

God's timing isn't always our timing, but instead of managing and manipulating our circumstances, we want to be aligned with his plans and purposes for our lives. No matter how desolate our future might look, with Christ there is always hope.

I have seen how God can turn around and restore some pretty dismal situations but, as the following story shows, it usually requires us to release—as in really let go of—our agenda and wait for his timing and guidance.

John dated Holly for over a year when she chose to end their relationship. He shared,

> It was hard to feel good about myself during that time. I not only lost Holly, but I lost my job because the company downsized, my mother passed away, and my teenage daughter from my previous marriage refused to talk to me or have anything to do with me.
>
> I didn't know where to go. My mind was whirling, my judgment was clouded, and all I could think of was Holly and how much I missed her. I had no income and no one in my life except my church friends. My sister lived hundreds of miles away and, although she wanted me to move near her, I knew changing my address wasn't going to solve my problems.

How easy it would have been for John to focus on all the negatives in his life and say, "Woe is me." However, he chose to seek wise counsel, trust God, and, as he says, "Instead of rearranging the chairs on the deck of the Titanic, I chose to do some real, hard work. I took a good look at myself, the issues that were driving me, and the self-defeating choices I kept making."

With counseling John discovered that for most of his life he'd been caught in the vicious cycle of performance. His identity had been firmly rooted in what he owned and what he could do for others. When he had to sell his home and move into a small apartment, he realized how hard he'd been working simply to be loved and accepted. He learned he needed to stop trying to be enough all the time. He began to grasp that with Christ he was loved for who he was rather than what he had or did.

"It was a frustrating time," John said, "but I grabbed hold of God and what I felt he was telling me to do. I prayed for the strength to keep going after Holly and I broke up, and then I just persevered."

John will be the first to tell you that going through those trials and dealing with his insecurities has given him joy and freedom, not to mention emotional and spiritual maturity he never would have had otherwise. "Looking backing I never thought my life could be so good." By the way, John not only found a job he loves, but after making some real changes within himself, he and Holly got back together and later married.

I'm not suggesting that when we confront a breakup there is always something we need to change in ourselves, or if we decide to work on ourselves we will find someone else immediately, or that we will get back with the person with whom we broke up. But I do believe it is important to take the time to do some self-analysis and consider if there are any issues we need to address or surrender to God. Too many singles rush into the next relationship before emotionally healing from the last. We want to not only identify any self-defeating behaviors we might have, but, like John, when everything is out of control we want to release it to God and follow his guidance.

The Challenge of Risking Again

"The reason I am so reluctant to date again," confessed one single woman, "is because it hurts too much when the relationship ends." If you're willing to put yourself out there in the dating world, it's a given fact that you are opening yourself up for the possibility of heartache and rejection. Sitting at home alone waiting for someone to fall into your lap is not much of an alternative.

> To love at all is to be vulnerable. Love anything, and your heart will certainly be wrung and possibly broken. If you want to make sure of keeping it intact, you must give your heart to no one, not even to an animal. Wrap it carefully round with hobbies and little luxuries; avoid all entanglements; lock it up safe in the casket or coffin of your

selfishness. But in that casket—safe, dark, motionless, airless—it will change. It will not be broken; it will become unbreakable, impenetrable, irredeemable...The only place outside Heaven where you can be perfectly safe from all the dangers...of love is Hell.[3]

When a relationship ends, it's a challenge to open ourselves up for possible pain and disappointment again—especially when we no longer have the invincible and idealistic mindsets of teenagers. When we've been deeply hurt after serious relationships, it's natural to want to protect ourselves. How do we find the courage to keep taking risks? How do we know which risks are worth taking?

Dr. Ben Carson says in *Take the Risk* that many people don't accomplish what they want because they are either afraid to take the risk or they take too many of the wrong risks. Taking too many of the wrong risks means allowing ourselves to get too close to someone too soon before we have a chance to know him or her. It means opening ourselves up for unhealthy relationships, such as with a controlling guy—like the man who took the menu out of the hands of my friend (on their first date no less) and said, "I've been observing you, and I know what you want. I'll take care of ordering your dinner."

While the Internet enables us to meet people we might never have crossed paths with otherwise, it also presents real risks—including the wrong kind. One of the biggest challenges of Internet dating is how easy it is to be deceived. When we meet someone in person, our radar normally flashes "Danger! Danger!" if we detect eye movements, tone of voice, or body language that is suspicious. When we meet someone online, we can't do that. "You can be duped so easily because you don't get the feedback you normally do when you interact with someone face-to-face," one friend said. "I sometimes feel like the Internet is a haven for unhealthy men. I mean you read all these intimate details about them, like what makes them smile and their favorite type of music, but it's more difficult to pick up on their real personalities or recognize if they have real character issues."

Another issue with Internet dating is that unless you live in or near a major city, your choices can be limited. And long-distance relationships have their own sets of risks. For example, how do you really get to know someone who lives thousands of miles away when you only spend a few exciting weekends together every now and then? One man who met his wife while traveling realized after they were married that their wonderful weekends together hadn't enabled him to see what she was really like on a daily basis.

Long-distance relationships aren't exposed to the reality of daily living, such as bad breath or body odor or someone being constantly late. These little irritations, while not fatal, can bring us back to earth in a hurry.

Whether we're talking about long-distance or Internet dating, one risk worth taking after several months of dating is to ask pointed questions. Two that will reveal a great deal of information are:

How do you describe our relationship to your friends and family?

What are you afraid I will find out about you and, as a result, like you less?

While there is no guarantee people will give us honest answers, we can often find out some pretty vital information simply by asking.

The Challenge of Needing Touch

Many of us singles wonder how to meet our needs for physical contact in *appropriate ways*. As healthy singles we can acknowledge our need for touch and accept responsibility for meeting it in a nonsexual, acceptable, and nonthreatening manner. By doing so we minimize the chances that we'll open ourselves up for self-destructive behaviors or troubled relationships.

One single woman I know volunteers at a local hospital, holding and rocking infants in the neonatal unit. Another woman says she schedules a massage every few weeks to fill her need for physical touch. Some people watch sporting events with others, enjoying the high fives and whacks on the shoulders when great plays occur.

And having a pet that meets you at the door, gives you kisses, or sits in your lap can counter coming home to an empty house.

Even when we successfully handle our need for physical touch, there is one aspect that can be a real temptation—sex.

The Challenge of Sexual Desire

We live in a sex-saturated culture. Everywhere we turn people are thinking about sex, talking about sex, and trying to get sex. We're taught that sex is necessary, indiscriminate sex is normal, sex is always great, and not having sex means we're ugly and unlovable. Is it any wonder that singles struggle with this issue?

How do we live month after month, year after year with the ongoing tension of handling our sexual longings in a godly way when it seems every movie, book, and TV show suggests we give in to them? Does sexual desire need to be satisfied? What do we do with this natural and strong drive? And this issue may be even more of a challenge if we've experienced sexual intimacy. "Some of my never-dated, never-been-kissed, never-did-anything friends seem to have it easier because they don't really know what they're missing," Laura said. "They see it on TV and elsewhere in the media, but without 'awakening love before it so desires,' they don't tend to worry about it so much."

It's About Connection

As singles, the most vibrant connections we can experience outside of marriage are not the result of physical intimacy but emotional and spiritual intimacy attained through close relationships with God and others. For example, we can connect intimately with others through empathy and service.

Selflessness connects us with others; selfishness disconnects us from others. As we consider and act on what is best for another person we feel good, we feel loving, we feel more connected, and we become more Christlike.

On the surface, some singles think that sexual intimacy "connects" them with other people. It does momentarily on a physical level. The problem is that, outside of a committed marital relationship, this short-term bond ends up being broken. Without taking the time to build trust and wait for real commitment, sooner or later the relationship ends and we become disconnected and experience great pain.

In fact, many singles say giving in to their desire for physical intimacy is why they ended up in destructive or difficult relationships. They wanted to be with someone or they gave in to their raging hormones and feelings of lust. They lost sight of the hurt their actions would cause or the feelings of guilt they would experience.

Author Rob Eagar writes that engaging in sexual activity before marriage is like using superglue. It bonds us to another person so tightly that we can't separate from them without causing damage to each other. If we repeat this physical intimacy with one partner after another, the continual ripping apart of our hearts will eventually numb our hearts, hindering our ability to experience real intimacy.[4]

As one single said, "I have been down this path and have made enough poor decisions that I know what the outcome will be. Knowing what will happen *before* I choose to have sex helps me to make better choices today."

It's About Discipline

In *Revelations of a Single Woman,* Connally Gilliam writes about sexual purity and says, "I think at some level there's simply an element of relentless struggle in this arena for someone who doesn't feel sexually shut down but is practicing celibacy."[5] It's this relentless struggle that needs to be recognized. We're not acknowledging it so we can feel sorry for ourselves, but we're acknowledging it so we can give voice to the discipline it takes to remain celibate in our society today. Like other spiritual disciplines, such as fasting, it can be difficult not to give in to our desires—especially during times of loneliness.

Choosing sexual purity means we intentionally connect with others in healthy, nonsexual ways. We're aware of what makes us most vulnerable to sexual temptation, and we make the choice to stay away from those situations as much as possible. I stay away from the mall on Saturday nights because I find myself focusing on all the couples who are shopping, and then I end up feeling alone and needy. I don't read romance novels because they remind me of what I don't have in my life (married friends tell me that's sometimes true of them also).

What makes you vulnerable, and how can you protect yourself from giving in to your sexual urges? One person I know who struggled in this area asked a friend to call her each day to see how she was doing at thinking and acting sexually pure. She said, "It enables me to stay on track."

What helps me is remembering that regardless of my marital status, I will experience unfulfilled desires and heartaches. For example, one married friend shared how much she admired Debbie, a godly Christian single who was still a virgin at 40. One Saturday Debbie spoke at my friend's church on how singles can stay sexually pure in today's world. During lunch my married friend and Debbie happened to be sitting together and both mentioned they hadn't slept well the night before. Debbie confided, "I was awake at three o'clock crying because I'm not married." Startled at the coincidence, my friend said, "I was awake at three o'clock crying because I *am* married."

The Challenge of Loneliness

Loneliness is probably the greatest struggle for singles. As my friend Jordan said, "There are those times that I wish I had someone to share the day with, to talk to about all that is going on, to go on trips together." Like Jordan, many times when I'm traveling I too yearn to have someone with me or someone to call and share the latest happenings with.

Sue, one of my close spiritual friends, has been married for years. Several months ago she was traveling alone on business. Because the singles she worked with were heavy on her heart, she asked God to give her insights into what it's like to be single. She said, "On my flight out to Nevada [she lives in Pennsylvania], there was no one sitting around me to talk to. During the five days I was there a business associate I was going to connect with cancelled. I never managed to talk with my husband on the phone because of my schedule and the time difference. One night I went to a show, and as I scanned the crowd all I could see were couples. I had no one to share the moment and say, 'Look at that or isn't that something.'"

On the flight home the lady sitting next to Sue got sick and spent most of her time in the restroom. That's when Sue definitely knew God had answered her prayer in an amazing way. By the time she saw her husband she was in tears. "It was a real eye-opener for me to experience the feelings that I did, looking at life as a single person for those few days," Sue said. "My heart is changed from the experience. I always figured it would be lonely, but I didn't realize how lonely it really was. And I'm sure God only gave me a glimpse."

At the beginning of this chapter I mentioned not embracing the idea that I could actually die single and happy. After wrestling with this issue and discussing it with a few single friends I resolved the matter. First, I realized I had equated single with being alone and lonely. I couldn't imagine myself dying lonely *and* happy. As Tracy, a woman in my singles group said, "There's a difference between dying single and dying alone and disconnected from others. You can die single but have lots of people in your life."

Vicki, a former singles ministry director, said it another way, "For me, the bigger picture is being in a relationship with Jesus and with others, and in remembering that this life isn't the end of the story. There's no guarantee how we will die, but when we hope in God and understand his bigger story, our lives in the present take on a different perspective."

Second, I realized part of the issue for me was wanting to be in control and be in charge of my future—including my death. I needed to surrender those desires to God (who is in charge) and accept I can't control how or when I'm going to die and whether or not I'm married when it happens. I also needed to accept that where I am right now is where God wants me. As the apostle Paul said, "Don't be wishing you were someplace else or with someone else. Where you are right now is God's place for you. Live and obey and love and believe right there. God, not your marital status, defines your life" (1 Corinthians 7:17 MSG).

Finally, I realized that how I die isn't as important as how I choose to live. As singles, it's important that we give voice to the struggles we face and accept our responsibility to handle them in a positive way. When things are beyond our control, such as whether we die married or single, we can surrender to God and ask him to change our hearts and the way we look at our circumstances.

Coaching Tip

We've discussed a few of the ongoing challenges of the single lifestyle and ways to handle our unmet needs and longings. In an effort to take responsibility for and find ways to meet your needs, consider which holidays you especially struggle with. How can you be more proactive in dealing with them? Planning ahead will make it less likely that you will seek someone or something unhealthy to ease your loneliness.

Once you've identified those times when you tend to be most vulnerable, fill in the details and then transfer them to your Smart Choice Relationship Profile. For example, you might plan to attend Christmas Eve services with family or a friend. On Valentine's Day, you could send cards to your closest friends and host a dinner for single friends.

Two Difficult Holidays and an Action Plan

This Christmas I will...

-

-

-

This Valentine's Day I will...

-

-

-

Live with Passion & Purpose

Who doesn't want to hang out with someone who lives passionately,
who loves fearlessly, and who embraces risk-laden change?[1]

BILL HYBELS

Many of us want to wait to buy homes or visit foreign countries until we have someone special to share the adventures with. Unfortunately, many years later we may still be waiting to do these things. All too often we put our lives on hold, believing that only a significant other, a spouse, or a child will give us a sense of purpose and the joy to live with passion. However, if we do this, we miss out on fully living right now. Waiting to live, believing we must have a significant other to share with, leads to feelings of dissatisfaction and neediness. As a result we might compromise our values and lose ourselves in the process of trying to find someone or something. Rather than waiting for life to begin or trying to get a different life, we need to start right now, right where we are, to live the life we've been given. A bonus is that this gives us more fulfilling lives to share!

As one single man commented about a recent blind date, "She doesn't like what she's doing, and she doesn't know what she wants to do with her life. She's a nice person, but I don't find her lack of direction really attractive. I'm not going to go out with her again." He made it very clear he's not attracted to someone with "no life." He's drawn to women who have a sense of purpose and meaning for their lives. Are you ready to step out and experience all life has to offer? Do you want to make some real changes? Where can you start?

Begin with God

The search for meaning begins with God. After all, he is the one who created us. "It is only in God that we discover our origin, our identity, our meaning, our purpose, our significance, and our destiny. Every other path leads to a dead end."[2] Each one of us is equipped with certain talents, strengths, and life experiences to do something no one else can do. As Paul reminds us, "We are God's workmanship, created in Christ Jesus to do good works, which God prepared in advance for us to do" (Ephesians 2:10).

The story of Joshua, who led the Israelites into the Promised Land after Moses died, illustrates how God prepares and equips us for the works he envisions. How was Joshua equipped? He was born into slavery in Egypt, and for the first part of his life he learned first-hand the impact of abusive, arrogant leaders, such as Pharaoh, who don't serve the one true God.

Joshua witnessed the miracles and power of God manifested through Moses as the Israelites were led out of Egypt and across the Red Sea. He experienced God's provision of food and water during their many years in the desert. As a military commander, Joshua led Israel to victory against the Amalekites. Most importantly, he was Moses' right-hand man for 40 years. Think of the valuable insights Joshua obtained about leadership—positive and negative—and the military experience he acquired over those years. Who else was so divinely designed to lead the Israelites?

In the same way, each one of us is being trained and given an education in areas so we will be distinctively qualified to do what God assigns us and make an eternal difference in the lives of others. The question is: Are we paying attention to God's hand in our lives? Have we taken the time to consider how he designed us?

Know Who You Are

When we take the time to know who we are, we are less likely to lose who we are. When we discover our uniqueness, we won't be as quick to change to please someone else. I'll never forget a friend in college who was willing to change her outgoing, spontaneous personality because her boyfriend didn't appreciate those traits. She said, "But if I don't change, I'll lose him forever." I looked at her in disbelief. "Don't you realize that if you do change for him you'll lose part of yourself—maybe forever?"

When we're clear that God created us as we are and is sculpting us to fulfill his will, we are less likely to end up being an "emotional amputee," someone who intentionally removes or allows others to remove a valuable part of herself to please or be accepted by others.

Author Michelle McKinney Hammond says that sometimes married women complain they've lost who they are after marriage. But the truth probably is that they never knew who they were in the first place—before they became a couple.

> Once a woman fully understands her purpose, she cannot misplace it unless she chooses to do so in exchange for a relationship with a man. When a woman fails to establish her identity, dissatisfaction causes her to say to her partner, "You are not making me happy." This statement, however, is a perversion of truth because, in actuality, the woman has made herself unhappy by not functioning according to her original design or purpose—or even taking the time to find out what it is. [3]

Unless we choose to know the person God meant us to be, we will feel empty and be merely existing. In contrast, when we live purposefully, we will experience a level of joy that we never knew possible and create attractive lifestyles worth sharing with others. One singles group created this list to describe the essence of someone who has a clear sense of purpose:

exciting	vibrant	enthusiastic
animated	dedicated	vivacious
dynamic	inspiring	full of life

Maybe you're like the person mentioned earlier—the direction-less date. You don't know what you want to do, but you're ready to make some changes. You're ready to discover God's plans and pur-poses for your life. Or maybe you're already working toward God's vision for your life. In either case, be willing to take the next step. Here are a few suggestions to guide you in your journey.

- find your passion
- seek God's perspective
- focus on your purpose
- rely on God's power
- expect a special pleasure

Find Your Passion

What Do You Care Deeply About?

The search for passion and purpose goes inward. Instead of listen-ing to those around you, take time to ask yourself and God, "What am I passionate about? What do I enjoy? What is meaningful to me?"

One of my passions is encouraging those who are overwhelmed by the circumstances in their lives and are experiencing a sense of hopelessness. Not only do I want to give them hope that they can grow through disappointing setbacks and devastating times, but I also want to teach those closest to the hopeless people how they can help and encourage people who are suffering.

My desire motivated me to start a syndicated radio feature enti-tled *The Mourning Glory Minute*. Each segment addresses a different topic, such as perseverance, giving listeners hope and encourage-ment to go on. One father of a terminally ill son wrote to me about the broadcast, "It enables me to 'keep on keeping on,' and reminds me I'm not the only one suffering in this world."

My passion of wanting to help the hopeless shows up in many

other areas of my life. Recently I was recording some training DVDs. Of the four topics I presented, there was one I couldn't wait to record. During the hours I worked on preparing and tightening this message, I kept thanking God for giving me the opportunity to use some horrible experiences in my life to make a difference in the lives of others. The message focused on specific ways we can help someone who is facing cancer. After filming the DVD of *Cancer: Seven Things You Need to Know to Help,* the producer commented on how obvious it was that this message came from a deep place inside me. One cameraman added, "Yeah…and it touched a very deep place in me."

What do you really care about? What's deep in your heart that can help others?

What Are Your Life Experiences?

God often uses some of our most painful or shameful experiences to enable us to make a significant difference in others. One example is this book. I didn't grow up dreaming that someday I would marry, divorce, and be single for years. However, as some of my friends and I struggled with learning the life skills of singleness and how to be reasonably well-adjusted, I've learned many valuable insights that I pass on through my life coaching and writing.

One of the defining moments for my friend Betsy was during her childhood when one of her sisters died. "We were never allowed to talk about her," Betsy said. "So no one knew how sad I was." Today she volunteers at Olivia's House, an organization committed to supporting grieving children. "We help children feel safe, and we help them express their feelings. Working with these children has filled up such a spot in my heart." Betsy's experiences drew her to Olivia's House and she continues to learn there as well. "It's not about me and my childhood memories. It's about focusing on the children and their pain. It's all about them."

What Are Your Skills, Talents, and Strengths?

What gifts has God given you? What are you especially good at? What areas do people compliment you on?

Brittany, divorced and in her late thirties, shared, "God has given me a lot of gifts, and I think the most important one is that I have an ability to relate to people easily. I have dealt with a lot of different people through my career, which has equipped me to be able to read people, understand them, and develop rapport easily. I'm using more of my time and my gifts to volunteer in organizations that are important to me."

About ten years ago I spent several days in the hospital after a surgical procedure. I met many nurses during that time. Karen was exceptionally gifted. Her competence, empathy, and tenderness promoted my healing. I'm certain her patients did better than other patients. One day I asked, "You love your job, don't you?"

"Oh, the hours zip by," she said. Then she told me that she was 45 years old and had been a teacher because that was what her mother wanted her to do. "I finally followed the dream God had tucked in my heart. Now I get to use all the abilities he's given me."

Whether you're gifted with children or gifted in music, use those strengths and talents! Research has shown there is a consistent correlation between using our strengths to help others and being happy. Some of the men at my church who are gifted in doing small repairs formed a handyman ministry. They tell everyone, "It's not what you get, but what you give that brings real joy."

Seek God's Perspective

After you've considered your passions, life experiences, skills, and gifts, pray for God's direction and guidance before rushing forward. "Many are the plans in a man's heart, but it is the LORD's purpose that prevails" (Proverbs 19:21).

There are times when God asks us to do something we don't feel passionate about and are not gifted in. Often in those moments we have to trust God in bigger leaps of faith. Only God can guide you in how to best spend your time and energy to make a real difference. And God's perspective isn't always our perspective (Isaiah 55:9). In the Old Testament we read of King David's passionate desire to build a temple for God. Doesn't that sound admirable? But God made it clear that while King David could *prepare* for building the temple, his son, Solomon, was to be the one to build it (2 Chronicles 6:7-10).

Our lives are part of a bigger story, a bigger plan. The sooner we align our lives with God's purposes, the sooner we'll be living for his glory and experience peace and contentment. If you're not certain what God is calling you to do, ask, "Is there an opportunity where I can serve others?" If we're only serving our own needs and interests, we're probably on the wrong path.

Sometimes to gain clarity we need to take the time to be still and listen to God. Maybe you're like author Ruth Haley Barton, who was told by a spiritual advisor that she was like a shaken-up jar of river water: "What you need is to sit still long enough so that sediment can settle and the water can become clear." [4]

The chaos and busyness of our lives keep the waters swirling within us, but when we allow ourselves to be still and listen for God's gentle whisper, we can often see his love and direction more clearly.

Focus on Your Purpose

We discussed the importance of focusing on God and his dreams for our lives. Once we have a clear understanding of his vision, we want to focus on making it a reality. Even with an unmistakable sense of purpose, it's easy to get caught up in the details of life and the desire to please others. If we don't intentionally focus on our purpose and readjust our priorities, we'll quickly lose sight of what's most important.

My friend's son was on leave from a tour of duty in Iraq with the Army. One afternoon as I chatted with Captain Johnathan, I asked what he'd learned from his experiences. "Before Iraq I had lost my focus in life," he said. "I've regained a sense of purpose. It's now crystal clear what's really important—Jesus."

I think, like Johnathan, when we understand how fragile our lives are, we get serious about using our time and talents wisely. When we are clear on God's vision for us, all our decisions are based on how best to use the resources we have been given in the time we have available.

My perennial question for my clients is, "What needs to grow…what needs to go?" Life contains many choices—some bad, but many are very good. Without a clear sense of what we need to nurture and what we need to discard, we will drift from one activity or relationship to another, often resulting in poor or mediocre decisions that rob us of the lives we were meant to have.

Rely on God's Power

We can't fulfill our God-given purpose in our own strength. We need God. He'll help us persevere in spite of our mistakes and setbacks, our times of discouragement and weariness, and our feelings of inadequacy.

In the book of Joshua, God reminded Joshua three times in the first nine verses to be strong and courageous. While we don't know exactly what was going through Joshua's mind at the time, we can conjecture that he was probably concerned about all the unknowns that lie ahead. For 40 years he'd been Moses' aide, and now Joshua was going to take the lead and do what Moses couldn't do—take the Israelites into the Promised Land. Joshua knew there were huge risks. He'd seen the giants of the land and knew they were real. The biblical warrior's life shows what God can do with someone who is obedient and willing to step out and take risks, even when he doesn't know exactly how it will turn out.

Joshua faced the giants and the towering walls of Jericho. What about you? Are you willing to face your giants, even when you don't know exactly *how* you're going to do something? As Andy Stanley says, "You will know what God has put in your heart to do before you know how he intends to bring it about. Often, you will know *what* long before you understand *how*." We need to remember that while the *how* might be a big problem for us it "is never a problem for God...*how* is God's specialty."[5]

Although he didn't always have a detailed battle plan, Joshua persevered as he led the Israelites in one battle after another. Sometimes God gave him a plan for a particular battle (see Joshua 6 and 8), but Joshua still needed to trust God and step out in faith. After seven years of fighting, the Israelites finally did settle in the Promised Land.

Expect a Special Pleasure

I continue to be amazed at what can happen when I stop trying to manage my life and let God use and shape me. It brings joy and fulfillment that is difficult to describe. Deep joy is a result of doing exactly what we were meant to do. As King Solomon wrote, "For he will not dwell unduly on the days of his life, because God keeps him busy with the joy of his heart" (Ecclesiastes 5:20 NKJV).

Don't get the idea that you have to do something extraordinary. One single said, "I love to entertain in my home." Another said she loves to be a good sounding board: "I hope people feel free to talk to me about anything." Whether you're leading a grief sharing group or praying for others, I pray you discover the joy of being part of something bigger than yourself.

So start living now! Stop putting your life on hold while you wait for romantic love. Stop waiting for a spouse or a child or a house to give you meaning and purpose. As therapist Jennifer Cisney says, "When we are living in the center of God's will, we don't have to have a romantic interest or spouse in our lives to be fulfilled. Our greatest joy comes from living out God's purpose."

When we live purposefully, we don't easily get bogged down with the problems in our lives. We won't be so intent on pursuing those who either aren't crazy about us or who aren't safe or healthy for us. We'll be too busy living our lives and focusing on the difference we can make. By following the passions of our hearts and the purposes of God, we will find the true riches of life!

Coaching Tip

As I was talking with a married friend about someone who was struggling to find meaning in her life, my friend said, "I just realized that the singles I most respect are those who are defined by something other than their marital status." (That should be true of married folks too.) Filling your life with purpose and meaning earns the respect of others and makes you a fascinating person. Start with your passions and take the time to discover what "is" you. Once while shopping I asked my friend for her opinion on a dress I tried on. "Oh, Georgia," she said, "you have to get it. That is so you!" And that is how we want to describe our passions and purposes: They are so us!

How has God designed you? What do you love to do? Think about when you were a child. What are the stories you love to tell? What gets you excited? Even if you don't know what you love (I didn't until the age of 40), don't give up. In God's time and in his way, he will reveal his plans.

Amazing Plans, by Martha Bolton

God has an amazing plan for your life…even when you're clueless.

God has an amazing plan for your life…even when you're scared.

God has an amazing plan for your life…even when others don't see it.

God has an amazing plan for your life…even when you think you're not qualified.

God has an amazing plan for your life…even when you wish He'd use someone else.

God has an amazing plan for your life…even when you think you don't deserve it.

God has an amazing plan for your life…even when you've wasted some of it.

God has an amazing plan for your life…even when it doesn't make sense.

God has an amazing plan for your life…even after you've let Him down.

And after you've let Him down again. And again. And again.

God has an amazing plan for your life…even when you're at your lowest.

God has an amazing plan for your life…even when you have a lesser plan.

God has an amazing plan for your life![6]

What are your passions? Maybe it's nature, encouraging others, or helping people realize their God-given dreams. Once you've identified your passions, write them down and add them to your Smart Choice Relationship Profile.

My Passions

-
-
-

Purpose, Protection, & Pals

Congratulations! You made it through the book and are ready to go forth with confidence, hope, and love. My prayer is that we stay away or get away from destructive relationships. As my friend Jennifer said, "I've been very fortunate in not dating any losers. In fact, I'm friends with everyone I've ever dated. Some say I'm picky, but I say I'm selective."

In the last chapter I mentioned Captain Johnathan Harvey. He told me that in Iraq the soldiers were taught to always go outside the compound with purpose, protection, and pals. This advice works for us too.

Purpose

Refuse to put your life on hold when you can make smart choices today. Instead of reacting to life, be intentional about being a healthy single. Christ needs to be the center of your life. With him you can face your fears and get outside your comfort zone. Take responsibility to wrestle, grieve over, and answer questions such as "What will my life look like if I never get married?" Be willing to do the hard work needed for growth and healing as you live with passion and purpose.

Protection

Protect yourself by listening to godly counsel. Guard yourself from negative feelings, thoughts, and lies that try to control or influence you. Read and gain knowledge on the differences between healthy and unhealthy relationships, between loving relationships and romantic ones. Use the wisdom of God found in Scripture and through the Holy Spirit to stay safe.

Pals

Being single does not mean living in isolation. Build and maintain a supportive social network. Be part of a community of people that includes close friends who accept you as you are and are willing to speak truth into your life. Find people who will cheer you on when you want to quit, settle for less than the best, or feel overwhelmed by the heavy burdens life sometimes brings. You need people to listen to you and inspire you to thrive and grow.

We don't know how long our season of singleness will last. So we need to make smart choices today and seize every opportunity to truly live. Remember, healthy, active singles are much more likely to attract other healthy, active singles!

8 Keys to Finding the Right Guy

To be a healthy, interesting, active single and to find the right guy, these parameters will help.

Wrestle with issues, grieve over what you need to, and answer life-changing questions that help you grow, such as "What will my life look like if I never get married?"

Cultivate caring relationships. Create a family of your own by building and maintaining a supportive social network.

Understand the difference between a loving relationship and a romantic one. Focus on what real love is rather than believing the myth that the "in love" feeling is *the* ultimate and will last forever.

Accept responsibility for meeting your desires and needs. Find appropriate ways to meet your need for physical touch and strong emotional connections. Plan ahead so difficult holidays won't be painful.

Face your fears and take risks. Get outside your comfort zone and take calculated risks. Refuse to be driven by your fears and any feeling of desperation.

Carve out time for cultivating your spiritual life. Make space and time for God. Recognize what's in your heart and be willing to do the work needed for growth and healing.

Serve others using your God-given gifts and experiences. Give of what you have—whether it be material possessions, talents, or lessons you've learned. Live with passion and purpose!

Realize Christ is your life. Know that only he can make you whole and love you unconditionally. He can provide peace and satisfaction.

Smart Choice Relationship Profile

Dating Inventory

Name	Attractive Qualities	Areas of Concern Noticed at Beginning	Negative Qualities Showed Over Time

My Deal Breakers

I will not continue to date someone who...

-

-

-

-

-

-

-

-

-

-

-

Three Fears That Influence My Relationships

1.

2.

3.

Three Blind Spots I've Ignored or Discounted

1.

2.

3.

Intimacy Blockers

_____

_____

_____

_____

_____

_____

_____

_____

_____

_____

_____

_____

_____

_____

_____

Despite What I Think and How I May Feel, Here's What God's Word Says Is True

Lie:

God's Truth:

Lie:

God's Truth:

Lie:

God's Truth:

Stress Relief Favorites

_____

_____

_____

_____

_____

_____

_____

_____

_____

_____

_____

_____

_____

_____

_____

My Style of Connecting with God

_____

_____

_____

_____

_____

_____

_____

_____

_____

_____

_____

_____

_____

_____

_____

_____

I'm Neglecting My Relationship with God When...

_____

_____

_____

_____

_____

_____

_____

_____

_____

_____

_____

_____

_____

_____

_____

My Social Network

-
-
-
-
-
-
-

My Closest Support

-
-
-
-

Top Five Deal-Makers

1.

2.

3.

4.

5.

Two Difficult Holidays and an Action Plan

This Christmas I will...

-

-

-

This Valentine's Day I will...

-

-

-

My Passions

_____

_____

_____

_____

_____

_____

_____

_____

_____

_____

_____

_____

_____

_____

_____

_____

_____

Notes

Chapter 1—Reflect on Your Dating History

1. Michael Cavanaugh, speaking at the Central Pennsylvania Regional Singles Conference, Living Word Community Church, York, PA, Nov. 14-15, 2003.

2. Phil McGraw, *Love Smart* (New York: Free Press, 2005), pp. 73-74.

3. Barbara DeAngelis, Ph.D, *Are You the One for Me? Knowing Who's Right & Avoiding Who's Wrong* (New York: Dell Publishing, 1992).

Chapter 2—Defeat the Fear Factor

1. Cheri Fuller, *Trading Your Worry for Wonder* (Nashville: Broadman & Holman, 1996), p. 9.

2. Catherine Marshall, *Adventures in Prayer* (New York: Ballantine Books, 1975), pp. 62-63.

3. Daniel Gilbert, *Stumbling on Happiness* (New York: Alfred A Knopf, 2006), p. 238.

Chapter 3—Recognize Blind Spots

1. Daniel Goleman, Ph.D., *Vital Lies, Simple Truths: The Psychology of Self-Deception* (New York: Simon & Schuster, 1985), p. 13.

2. Richard Nelson Bolles, quoted in David Goetz and editors of Christianity Today International, *Leadership Devotions: Cultivating a Leader's Heart* (Wheaton, IL: Tyndale House Publishers, Inc., 2001), p. 6.

3. Goleman, *Vital Lies, Simple Truths*, p. 15.

4. Dwight Bain, personal conversation with author.

5. Jennifer Roback Morse, *Smart Sex: Finding Life-Long Love in a Hook-Up World* (Dallas, TX: Spence, 2005).

6. Kate Fraher, "Is Sex Making Students Sick?" IMFC Review, Spring/Summer, 2007, p. 7.

7. Daniel Gilbert, *Stumbling on Happiness* (New York: Alfred A. Knopf, 2006), p. 229.

Chapter 4—Minimize Dating Disasters

1. Madeleine L. Van Hecke, *Blind Spots: Why Smart People Do Dumb Things* (Amherst, NY: Prometheus Books, 2007), p. 239.

Chapter 5—Overcome a Less-Than-Stellar Family

1. W. Hugh Missildine, quoted in Josh McDowell, *His Image, My Image* (San Bernardino, CA: Here's Life Publishers, Inc., 1984), pp. 52-53.

2. Abigail Trafford, "Making the Most of Life, Even Without a Perfect Childhood," *The Washington Post*, May 22, 2007, HE04.

3. Philip A. Cowan, quoted in ibid.

Chapter 6—Know and Live the Truth

1. *Original Sin*, MGM, directed by Michael Cristofer, produced by Sheldon Abend, Ashok Amritrzj, David Hoberman, © 2001, based on Cornell Woolrich, *Waltz into the Darkness*. Antonio Bandaras and Angelina Jolie star, and this film certainly deserves its R rating for strong sexual content and violence.

2. Ruth Myers, *The Satisfied Heart: 31 Days of Experiencing God's Love* (Colorado Springs: Waterbrook Press, 1999), pp. 2-3.

3. Ibid., p. 6.

4. Joanna Weaver, *Having a Mary Heart in a Martha World* (Colorado Springs: Waterbrook Press, 2000), p. 26.

Chapter 7—Convert Pain to Positive Change

1. Larry Crabb, *Shattered Dreams* (Colorado Springs: Waterbrook Press, 2001), p. 85.

2. Kyle Almoney, © 2004, used by permission.

Chapter 8—Cultivate Your Inner Life

1. Ruth Myers, *The Satisfied Heart: 31 Days of Experiencing God's Love* (Colorado Springs: Waterbrook Press, 1999), pp. 34-35.

2. Julie Fehr, quoted in Joy Jacobs and Deborah Strubel, *Single, Whole and Holy: Christian Women and Sexuality* (Camp Hill, PA: Horizon Books, 1996), pp. 207-08.

3. Henri Nouwen, *The Wounded Healer* (New York: Doubleday, 1972), p. 85.

4. Gary Thomas, *Sacred Pathways: Discover Your Soul's Path to God* (Nashville: Thomas Nelson Publishers, 1996), p. 17.

5. Oswald Chambers, *My Utmost for His Highest* (Grand Rapids, MI: Discovery House Publishers, 1992), p. 28.

6. Richard Exley, *The Other God: Seeing God As He Really Is* (Plainfield, NJ: Logos International, 1979), pp. 33-34.

7. Erwin Raphael McManus, *The Barbarian Way: Unleash the Untamed Faith Within* (Nashville: Thomas Nelson, 2005), p. 31.

Chapter 9—Build a Supportive Community

1. Janet Kornblum, "Study: 25% of Americans have no one to confide in," *USA Today*, June 23-25, 2006, p. 1A.

2. David Brooks, "The New Lone Rangers," *New York Times*, July 10, 2007, op-ed.

3. Eugene Peterson, *Christ Plays in Ten Thousand Places: A Conversation in Spiritual Theology* (Grand Rapids, MI: William B. Eerdmans Publishing Co., 2005), p. 226.

4. Daniel Goleman, *Social Intelligence: The New Science of Human Relationships* (New York: Bantam Dell, 2006), p. 20.

5. John M. Gottman, Ph.D., *The Relationship Cure* (New York: Three Rivers Press, 2001), p. 6.

6. Henry Cloud, "The Doctor Is In," *Christian Single*, March 2003, p. 20.

Chapter 10—Choose Character over Chemistry

1. John Van Epp, *How to Avoid Marrying a Jerk* (New York: McGraw Hill, 2006), p. 3.

2. M. Scott Peck, *The Road Less Traveled* (New York: Simon & Schuster, 1978), pp. 84-85.

3. Ibid., p. 89.

4. D.L. Moody, quoted in Charles L. Wallis, ed., *The Treasure Chest* (New York: Harper & Row, 1965), p. 46.

5. John Gottman, quoted in Daniel Goleman, *Emotional Intelligence* (New York: Bantam Dell, 1994), pp. 134-35.

6. John M. Gottman and Joan DeClaire, *The Relationship Cure* (New York: Three Rivers Press, 2001), p. 4.

7. Chambers, *My Utmost for His Highest*, March 28.

8. Jason Illian, excerpted from "Undressed: The Naked Truth About Love, Sex, and Dating," 2006 SinglesNewsletter@ChristianityToday.com, October 11, 2006.

9. Phil McGraw, *Love Smart* (New York: Free Press, 2005), p. 29.

Chapter 11—Manage the Ongoing Challenges

1. Thomas Huxley, quoted in Charles L. Wallis, ed., *The Treasure Chest* (New York: Harper & Row, 1965), p. 83.

2. Ronald Rolheiser, *Forgotten Among the Lilies: Learning to Live Beyond Our Fears* (New York: Doubleday, 2005), p. 51.

3. C.S. Lewis, *The Four Loves,* quoted in John and Stasi Eldredge, *Captivating* (Nashville: Thomas Nelson, 2005), p. 182.

4. Rob Eagar, *Dating with Pure Passion* (Eugene, OR: Harvest House, 2002), p. 128.

5. Connally Gilliam, *Revelations of a Single Woman* (Carol Stream, IL: Tyndale House, 2006), p. 68.

Chapter 12—Live with Passion & Purpose

1. Bill Hybels, *Holy Discontent: Fueling the Fire That Ignites Personal Vision* (Grand Rapids, MI: Zondervan, 2007), p. 126.

2. Rick Warren, *The Purpose Driven Life* (Grand Rapids, MI: Zondervan, 2002), p. 18.

3. Michelle McKinney Hammond, *How to Make Love Work* (New York: FaithWorks, 2007), pp. 70-71.

4. Ruth Haley Barton, "Beyond Words: An Invitation to Solitude and Silence," *Conversations: A Forum for Authentic Transformation,* vol. 5:2, Fall/Winter 2007, p. 8.

5. Andy Stanley, *Visioneering* (Sisters, OR: Multnomah, 1999), pp. 55-56, emphasis added.

6. Martha Bolton, "Amazing Plans." Used by permission.

About the Author

Georgia Shaffer knows all too well what it's like to date the wrong guy, but she also knows what is needed to experience the joys of healthy relationships. She is passionate about coaching singles and young adults to be thoughtful about making smart choices. As a licensed psychologist in Pennsylvania and a certified life coach, Georgia established SingleLife Coaching (www.SingleLifeCoaching.com) to provide one-on-one support for those who want to grow, live life fully, and find lasting love.

Georgia is a regular columnist for *Christian Coaching Today* and a board member of the International Christian Coaches Association (ICCA). She's the author of *Taking Out Your Emotional Trash: Face Your Feelings and Build Healthy Relationships, A Gift of Mourning Glories: Restoring Your Life After Loss,* and for Christian Coaches she's compiled the experiences and stories of 49 coaches for the book *Coaching the Coach: Life Coaching Stories and Tips for Transforming Lives.* She has spoken to thousands of people across the country. She's appeared on *The 700 Club, Decision Today,* and Sky Angel's *A Time for Hope.*

Her story and photos are featured in the film *Letters to God* and she is part of the *Women of Extraordinary Faith DVD.* Georgia has also shared her expertise in DVD series for the American Association of Christian Counselors such as *Professional Life Coaching 101, 201, Advanced Life Coaching;* Hope Coaching and Divorce Recovery. Additionally she is featured in *Jesus—Fact or Fiction? Tough Questions, Compelling Answers.* This DVD, produced by Campus Crusade, is a companion to *The Jesus Film* and includes Georgia's testimony and her participation in a question-and-answer format with Lee Strobel, Josh McDowell, Ravi Zacharius, and others.

When she isn't speaking or writing, Georgia loves to work in her garden and spend time with her family.

For free resources, including a
downloadable Smart Choice Relationship Profile,
to sign up for Georgia's newsletter, or
to invite her to speak to your group, visit

www.GeorgiaShaffer.com.